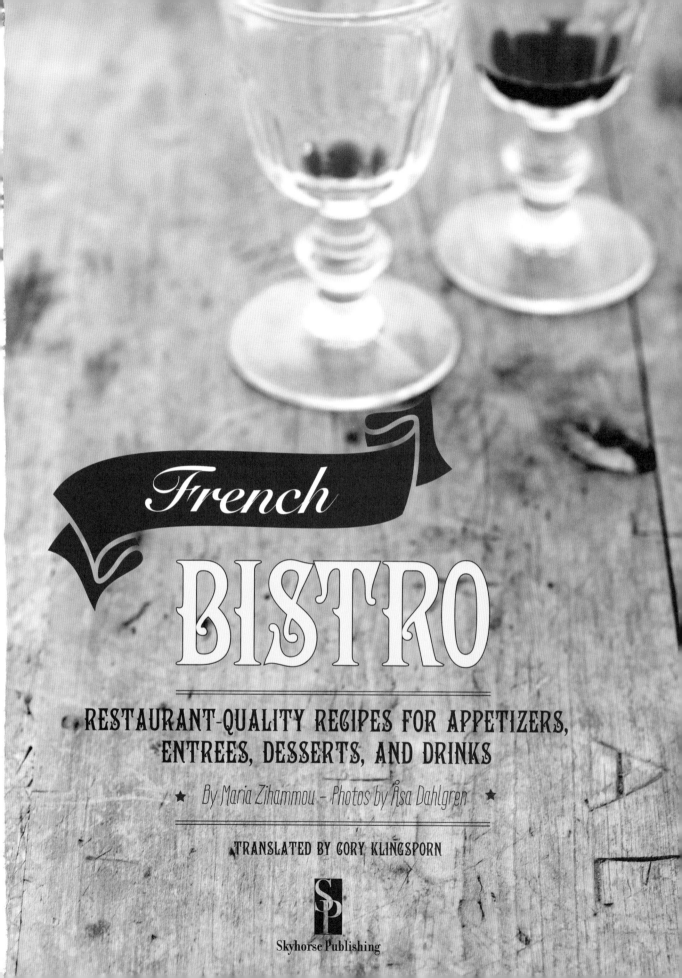

French

BISTRO

RESTAURANT-QUALITY RECIPES FOR APPETIZERS, ENTREES, DESSERTS, AND DRINKS

★ By Maria Zihammou – Photos by Åsa Dahlgren ★

TRANSLATED BY CORY KLINGSPORN

Skyhorse Publishing

TABLE OF CONTENTS

Copyright © 2013 by Maria Zihammou
English Translation © 2014 by Skyhorse Publishing
First published in 2013 as Fransk bistro by Maria Zihammou, Bokförlaget Semic, Sundbyberg, Sweden
Photography by Åsa Dahlgren
Graphic design by Monica Sundberg

Skyhorse Publishing books may be purchased in bulk at special discounts for sales promotion, corporate gifts, fund-raising, or educational purposes. Special editions can also be created to specifications. For details, contact the Special Sales Department, Skyhorse Publishing, 307 West 36th Street, 11th Floor, New York, NY 10018 or info@skyhorsepublishing.com.
Skyhorse® and Skyhorse Publishing® are registered trademarks of Skyhorse Publishing, Inc.®, a Delaware corporation.
www.skyhorsepublishing.com
10 9 8 7 6 5 4 3 2 1
Library of Congress Cataloging-in-Publication Data is available on file.
Print ISBN: 978-1-62873-645-8
Ebook ISBN: 978-1-62914-958-5
Printed in China

Bonjour, ça va?

If there's one thing I love more than anything, it's food that is tied to a beautiful feeling. Food that evokes memories of trips when I tasted my way and discovered new dimensions in an ingredient. This is how life has always been for me. I am able to remember a taste from a trip, and it inspires me to make new dishes my own way, at home in my kitchen, to regain that beautiful feeling.

When I visited France for the first time, it was by InterRail. I tasted sweet nectarines and melons in Nice. Munched on small, black olives with a nutty flavor, and ate pissaladière filled with sweet onion, olives, and anchovies at a small bakery. I wrinkled my nose at steak tartare but instead tried a wonderful soupe de poisson in Aix-en-Provence. I sought out simple bistros in Paris and enjoyed French onion soup and crème brûlée for dessert. Trying food that makes my taste buds rejoice makes for an experience that lingers in my mind for a good, long while . . .

It's easy to like French bistro food. It's food that is unpretentious and well-made. The waiters dance around the tables, swinging their trays graciously through the air, and deftly set the food on the table. That's what a bistro is to me.

In "French Bistro," you'll find my personal interpretations of favorite French classics and modern spins on various regional dishes: Asparagus with egg and lemon, pot-au-feu, lavender chicken, warm goat cheese salad with rosemary and apples, and fabulous pears simmered in red wine. Doesn't that sound delicious?

I hope that you'll experience how fun it is to make bistro food. With the help of my recipes, you can create the French bistro feeling right in your own home.

Bon appétit!

C'est moi qui l'ai fait!

The French take great pride in their regional traditions-the cultured and the refined, in their own terroir. I enjoy it to the fullest when I visit a market and get close to the people who are there to sell their wares. Talk to the small, plump cheesemonger. Taste her cheeses, and get tips on which ones go best with what. Try different kinds of butter-there really is more than one kind! Smell your way through the stands packed with fruits and vegetables. Be captivated by the beauty of a fresh artichoke. Buy wine from the winemaker who can't stop talking about his creations, which he would like you to taste.

This is a good place to start, with good ingredients of high quality. I want to tantalize your taste buds and lead you to discover how wonderfully delicious French food is. I know! We often ate French food at home when I was growing up. Mama made garlic-fried mushrooms and vegetables simmered in good broth-à la Grecque. Or Papa would cook herring with garlic and parsley. In French Bistro, I've gathered together all of my personal favorites.

Food that tastes good makes you happy. A quick, simple lunch should taste just as good as a festive holiday dinner. But when there are celebrations involved, you take your time and sit for a while, allowing yourself to eat and make merry. A French holiday meal always starts with an amuse-bouche and apéritif. Then you have appetizers, entrées, cheese, and dessert. And at the very end, a digestif. Now, let's get started!

AMUSE-BOUCHES
("mouth entertainers")

APPETIZERS

Sometimes, I like to entertain my guests with a delicious snack before dinner. A few olives and a glass of wine can be the quickest way to put together an appetizer. Amuse-bouche means "mouth entertainer," and entertaining the mouth is exactly what all cooking is about, if you ask me.

Add a nice sausage to the olives on a cutting board and a freshly baked pain au levain or baguette. If you're hungry for something that takes a bit more work, I'd say you ought to try rilettes, or oysters with sherry and spinach. A plate with different amuse-bouches, where you've collected different flavors—some savory, some sweet, and some tart—together with an apéritif is a simple way to hold a small get-together. Skip dinner and do things the way they're done in France, where people are happy to socialize and eat a few different morsels with a good drink. Ready your taste buds, and enjoy.

7

"Start with the best of the best—a glass of ice-cold champagne."

★ *HUÎTRES VARIÉES* ★

OYSTERS: THREE WAYS

4 PEOPLE

Oysters taste naturally of the ocean and are easy to eat, but difficult to open. Sample oysters just as they are or with a vinaigrette. They're also good to toss in the oven with garlic butter or with sherry, cream, and spinach as is shown here. My friend Per Karlsson in Grebbestad has taught me both how to love oysters and how to open them. Pour off the water inside and don't forget to chew!

6 oysters per person

WITH VINAIGRETTE

1 shallot
3½ tbsp (50 ml) sherry vinegar or red wine vinegar
a pinch of salt
a pinch of freshly ground black pepper

➤ To make the vinaigrette, start by peeling and mincing the shallot. Combine with the vinegar, salt, and freshly-ground pepper. Serve in a bowl beside the oysters. When it's time to eat, spoon a teaspoon of the vinaigrette over a freshly opened oyster and enjoy with a glass of champagne.

AU GRATIN WITH GARLIC BUTTER

3½ tbsp (50 g) butter, room temperature
1 garlic clove
1 tbsp finely chopped parsley
a pinch of salt

➤ Preheat the oven to 475°F (250°C); or broil. Place the butter in a bowl. Peel and mince the garlic. Mix the butter, garlic, parsley and salt together.
➤ Open each oyster, remove the top shell, and pour out any extra liquid. Put a dollop of garlic butter on each oyster and place them in a dish. Brown at the upper part of the oven for one minute.

AU GRATIN WITH SHERRY AND SPINACH

½ cup (100 ml) cream
1 tbsp dry sherry
a pinch of salt
a pinch of freshly ground black pepper
½ cup (100 ml) fresh spinach

➤ Preheat the oven to 475°F (250°C), broil. Pour the cream and sherry into a casserole dish. Sprinkle with salt and pepper. Cook until the liquid is reduced by half.
➤ Stir the spinach into the cream. Open each oyster, remove the top shell, and pour out any extra liquid. Add about a tablespoon of the sherry cream to each oyster. Place in a dish, and brown at the top of the oven for one minute.

TAPENADE

Savory and rich, tapenade is perfect on a slice of baguette. Take a black olive and remove the pit. This can be done easily by placing the olive on a cutting board and pressing with your thumb until the pit pops out. Tapenade tastes best when you use olives with pits.

4 people

10½ oz (300 g) black olives with pits
1 garlic clove
1 tbsp finely chopped parsley
1 tbsp lemon juice
1 tsp Dijon mustard
3½ tbsp cup (50 ml) xtra virgin olive oil
salt and freshly ground black pepper

➤ Remove the pits from the olives and peel the garlic. Place the olives, garlic, parsley, lemon juice, Dijon mustard, and olive oil in a mixer. Blend to desired texture. Add a little bit of salt and freshly ground pepper to taste.

FRESH CHEESE WITH HONEY AND APRICOT

Oh, how I love this appetizer. It's the combination of the tart fresh cheese with a pinch of sea salt and the sweetness of the honey and apricots that make this dish simply irresistible. It's easy to throw together and can be served with a baguette and rosé wine.

4 people

1¼ cup (300 ml) thick yogurt
¾ cup (200 ml) crème fraîche or sour cream
approx. 1 tsp sea salt flakes
1 tbsp honey
6 apricots, coarsely shredded
baguette, for serving

➤ Warm the yogurt and crème fraîche in a pan. Stir until the mixture reaches 100°F (37°C), or until it's hot to the touch. Pour into a cheesecloth and let the mixture drain for about two hours. Place the cheese into the refrigerator and let cool.

➤ Shortly before serving, stir the cheese in a bowl with a spoon until it reaches a creamy consistency. Place on a serving dish. Sprinkle with sea salt flakes, drizzle with honey, and top with coarsely shredded apricots. Serve with the baguette.

ONION CONFIT

Crispy, sweet-and-sour onions pair beautifully with a slice of pâté. Choose small, pearl onions and simmer them with sugar, honey, and fruity red wine. Add a few sprigs of thyme and you'll have a lovely onion confit, which should keep for at least a week in the fridge.

4 people

12 pearl onions
2 tbsp butter
2 tbsp raw sugar
1 tbsp honey
¾ cup (200 ml) red wine
1 tbsp finely chopped thyme
a pinch of sea salt flakes

➤ Peel the onions. Chop larger onions into chunks or halves. Heat the butter in a pan and lightly brown the onions.

➤ Pour into a saucepan and add the sugar, honey, wine, thyme, and salt. Simmer while covered until the onions are soft and most of the liquid has been absorbed.

➤ Place in thoroughly cleaned bowls. Serve alongside cold cuts or pâté with bread and salad.

PÂTÉ WITH RADISHES AND HORSERADISH CREAM

I ate this simple dish at La Marlotte in Paris. The dish is centered around a proper slice of delicious pâté. The rain poured down on the other side of the window, and it was wonderful to sit in that fine restaurant while being pampered. You don't have to slice the radishes into a rose, but it certainly looks beautiful on the plate. Typical French bistro fare!

★ ★ ★ ★ ★

4 people

4 slices of good pâté
1 bunch of radishes
4–8 gherkins
baguette, for serving

Horseradish cream:
¾ cup (200 ml) whipping cream
3½ tbsp (50 ml) grated horseradish
½ tsp salt

➥ Place pâté slices on four small plates.

➥ Rinse the radishes, and dry them with a kitchen towel. With a sharp knife, make six shallow cuts around each radish, just beneath the skin. Go around the radishes once again, making six more slits underneath the first ones. Place the radishes in a bowl of ice water, and allow them to sit for a while so they open up.

➥ Partially slice through the gherkins lengthwise, making sure they still remain in one piece. Apply light pressure with one hand so they spread out like fans.

➥ Whip the cream until fluffy, and mix in the horseradish and salt Serve the pâté with the radishes, gherkins, horseradish cream, and baguette.

PORK RILLETTES

Slowly baked meat, simmered in a casserole dish in the oven until it falls apart, is called rillettes in France. Pieces of tenderloin and pork belly simmer together with herbs and wine to create a wonderful texture and flavor. Fill bowls with rillettes and top with oil, and store in the fridge. Best enjoyed slowly with bread and tart gherkins or cornichons.

2 jars

1 lb (500 g) fresh pork belly
1 lb (500 g) pork tenderloin
4 garlic cloves
1 small bunch of thyme sprigs
1 tbsp finely minced thyme
2 bay leaves
2 whole cloves
¼ tsp ground nutmeg
½ cup (100 ml) white wine or dry cider
water
salt and freshly ground black pepper
½ cup (100 ml) olive oil, for drizzling
bread and gherkins when serving

☞ Preheat the oven to 300°F (150°C). Slice the meat into smaller pieces. Peel the garlic and tie the thyme sprigs with cooking twine. Toss all of this into a casserole dish or other oven-safe dish, and add the finely shredded thyme, bay leaves, cloves, nutmeg, and white wine or cider. Fill with enough water to cover. Cover the dish with a lid.

☞ Leave the dish in the oven for three hours. Read a book, or engage in some other pleasant activity! Remove the dish from the oven and allow it to simmer on the stove until the meat is so tender it falls apart, which should take about 30–40 minutes. Scoop the meat out with a slotted spoon and place it in a bowl where it can cool off a bit. Remove the bay leaves, thyme, and cloves. Beat with an electric mixer until the meat reaches a stringy consistency. Add salt and pepper to taste. Place in thoroughly cleaned jars. Press down the rillettes to remove any air. Cover with a layer of olive oil or melted lard. Keeps for up to a month in the fridge.

☞ Serve with grilled sourdough bread and gherkins, or cornichons.

SALMON RILLETTES

A variant on rillettes made with both fresh and smoked salmon. Good in a picnic basket or as a snack before dinner. Bake the salmon in the oven until it becomes nice and juicy. Then add the smoked salmon, lemon, and fresh herbs.

2 jars

10½ oz (300 g) salmon fillet, without skin
a pinch of salt
2 tbsp butter
2 tbsp dry white wine
2 tbsp extra virgin olive oil
½ organic lemon, zest and juice
a small bunch of chives
a small sprig of dill
7 oz (200 g) smoked salmon
a pinch of cayenne pepper
salt and freshly ground black pepper
bread, for serving

☞ Preheat the oven to 300°F (150°C). Season the salmon with salt. Butter a pan and place the salmon in it. Pour the wine over top. Bake the salmon for 15–20 minutes or until it falls apart easily when poked carefully with a fork. Allow the salmon to cool a bit.

☞ Pour the olive oil and lemon juice into a bowl, along with the lemon zest. Finely chop the chives and dill, and stir in the smoked salmon. Mash with a fork before adding the oven-baked salmon. Mix and season with cayenne pepper, salt, and black pepper. Season to the preferred saltiness.

☞ Distribute into two thoroughly cleaned jars and store in the fridge, where it should keep for at least one week. Serve on sourdough bread or slices of baguette.

FOIE GRAS MOUSSE WITH FIGS

There can be no doubt about the luxury and allure of foie gras mousse. Best of all, this appetizer is incredibly easy to make. I think it is most delicious when served with champagne.

4 people

7 oz (200 g) foie gras mousse
2 brioches
2 tbsp butter
2 tbsp fig spread
2 fresh or dried figs

➤ Slice the foie gras mousse into smaller pieces.
➤ Cut off the top and bottom of the brioches. Cut each into three or four slices. Next, cut each slice first in half, then into quarters. Warm the butter in a pan and fry the bread until golden on both sides.
➤ Place the brioche on a serving dish and put a piece of the foie gras mousse on each slice. Top with fig spread. Slice the figs into small wedges and place them on top of each piece.
➤ If you can't find brioche, you can serve the mousse on thinly sliced baguette, fried in butter just as the brioche is here.

LOBSTER SKEWERS WITH GREEN GRAPES

To bring out the natural sweetness found in lobsters, I've chosen to combine them with something tart. Green grapes with fresh lobster tails are really quite delicious.

4 people
4 fresh lobster tails
1 small bunch of green grapes

➤ After cooking the lobster, remove it from its shell and cut each tail into four pieces. Place on toothpicks with a grape.

18

CHEESE BALLS WITH ROQUEFORT AND CELERY

If you don't like Roquefort, you can substitute any other fresh cheese for it and prepare the dish in the same way. Natural cheese curd products taste the best, seasoned however you like. They're delicious with a pinch of cayenne pepper and a touch of orange zest. Cool the cheese and roll the balls in parsley.

4 people

7 oz (200 g) Roquefort
(or any other type of fresh cheese)
3½ tbsp (50 g) butter, room temperature
1 tbsp cognac
1 pinch salt
2 tbsp finely chopped celery
¼ cup (50 ml) finely chopped parsley

☞ Mash the cheese with a fork in a deep dish. Mix in the butter. Add the cognac, salt, and the chopped celery. Form into round balls, about the size of walnuts. Roll them in parsley.

MARINATED OLIVES

When I was in Nice many years ago, I couldn't get enough of their small black olives. I bought a bag of them at the market and snacked on them with bread and a bit of cheese. They have a nutty flavor that's unbelievably tasty. I made several more trips to that market!

BLACK, WITH HERBES DE PROVENCE

Season black olives with southern French herbs. Herbes de Provence is a mixture of several herbs, like thyme, rosemary, basil, and marjoram. These olives are delightful with freshly cooked lamb or with bread, cheese, and wine for a simple picnic. Eating delicious food outdoors might be the best thing there is!

½ cup (100 ml) black olives with pits, (preferably Nice olives)
1 tbsp Herbes de Provence
2 tbsp extra virgin olive oil

☞ Mix the olives, herbs, and oil in a bowl. Pour into a jar and let the olives sit for a while, preferably overnight, to develop the flavor. Serve with aperitifs, or on the side with grilled lamb cutlets.

GREEN, WITH LEMON

If you're lucky enough to come across a jar of Lucques olives from Languedoc, try marinating them with lemon and olive oil. These olives are heavenly. They have a buttery flavor and a light lemon aftertaste. Whatever kind you use, what's most important is to use olives that still have their pits. They're the perfect snack to pair with an aperitif before your meal!

½ cup (100 ml) green olives with pits
1 organic lemon
2 tbsp extra virgin olive oil

☞ Place the olives in a bowl. Zest half of the lemon, avoiding the white pith, which tastes bitter. Squeeze out the lemon juice, add oil, and stir. Pour into the bowl with the olives and serve before dinner or with oven-baked chicken. If you have time, prepare the olives one day in advance so the flavor has time to develop.

GREEN, WITH FENNEL

A glass of pastis and these olives make for a fine, fine combination. If you can, prepare the olives at least a day before eating them. That way, the flavors will have enough time to develop fully.

½ cup (100 ml) green olives with pits
¼ fresh fennel bulb
1 tsp fennel seeds
1 tbsp lemon juice
2 tbsp extra virgin olive oil

☞ Place the olives in a bowl. Cut the fennel into thin slices. Add the fennel and fennel seeds, lemon juice, and olive oil to the bowl. Stir, and pour into jars with tight-fitting lids, and allow them to marinate, preferably overnight. Store in the fridge.

MUSHROOMS WITH GARLIC AND PARSLEY

*This is unbelievably tasty and easy to make. To me. it smells like childhood.
My mom used to make this dish when I was little. served on crisp bread.
Imagine crunchy homemade crackers with warm. freshly cooked mushrooms
on top. That's what I call an evening snack!*

4 servings

8 oz (225 g) mushrooms
2 garlic cloves
1 tbsp butter
1 tbsp extra virgin olive oil
2 tbsp finely chopped parsley
salt and black pepper
homemade crackers or crisp bread,
for serving

☛ Rinse and slice the mushrooms. Peel and mince the garlic. Warm
the butter and oil in a pan. Quickly sauté the mushrooms, and add the
garlic when almost all the liquid has evaporated. Don't sauté the garlic
any longer than one minute, as it burns easily and will taste bitter.
☛ Remove from the heat, and add parsley. Season with salt and
pepper. Serve immediately on crackers.

Bistrot

IN A MINUTE

No doubt there have been many times where you didn't know what to make for dinner. Flipping through recipes without really finding anything because everything seemed too troublesome and time-consuming. Sometimes, the ingredient list alone is who-knows-how-long! The stew's supposed to be made the day before, and the bread needs sourdough and yeast to sit for two days.

Then there are days when you've got neither the time nor the inclination to be in the kitchen. Sometimes, things have got to be quick! If you're tired and stressed out, make something simple and easy. There's always a way to prepare something tasty. An omelet with cheese and herbs, a flavorful salad, mussel stew, or the classic bœuf à la minute. Regardless of what you choose, the result will always turn out delicious if you choose ingredients that are of high quality and in season.

MINUTE STEAK WITH FRENCH HERBS AND SALAD

This is a simple and quick French bistro favorite that I love to make. But I'm always careful with what sort of meat I choose. Look for a steak that's nicely marbled, preferably from a butcher who knows his stuff. Serve the steak seasoned with Herbes de Provence, salad, and baguette. Simple and so delicious!

★ ★ ★ ★ ★

4 PEOPLE

*4 nicely marbled, room temperature
sirloin steaks (each ½ lb / 200 g)
salt and freshly ground black pepper
1 + 1 tbsp butter
2 tbsp olive oil
1–2 tbsp Herbes de Provence*

SALAD

*1 head of lettuce
1 bag of baby greens
2 tbsp red wine vinegar
1 tbsp lemon juice
4 tbsp extra virgin olive oil
salt and pepper
bread, for serving*

· Start with the salad: rinse and separate the lettuce leaves, then break them apart into smaller pieces. Mix the vinegar, lemon juice, and oil in a bowl, and season to taste with salt and pepper. Put in the leaves and toss thoroughly.

· Lightly tenderize the steaks with a mallet. Season with salt and pepper on both sides. Heat a pan with a tablespoon of butter and oil. Place the meat in the pan once the butter has settled down and pan-fry for about two minutes on each side, depending on how well done you like your steak. I like my steak juicy with a red center, so I usually feel the steaks to make sure they're still nice and tender. They ought to be soft in the middle—that's when I think they're perfect.

· Remove the meat and place it in a plate. Sprinkle with French herbs, and deglaze the pan with two tablespoons of water and one tablespoon of butter. Pour this over the steaks. Serve with the salad and bread.

MINI LÉGUMES ET JAMBON CRU

BABY VEGETABLES WITH HAM

Here, freshly harvested baby vegetables are the star, along with a fresh vinaigrette and slices of finely cooked or smoked ham. I was served this at a bistro that became my favorite on the *rue du Cherche-Midi* in Paris. Don't cook the vegetables too long! They should be soft, but not too mushy.

★ ★ ★ ★ ★

4 PEOPLE

1 bunch of green asparagus
1 small squash
1 bunch of onions
1 bunch of baby carrots
salt

VINAIGRETTE

3 tbsp extra virgin olive oil
½ lemon, juice
1 pinch salt

ALONG WITH

7 oz (200 g) cooked or smoked
ham, of high quality
bread and butter

• Trim the asparagus and cut away the bottoms, which tend to be woody. Slice the squash into oblong wedges. Cut away a bit of the onion tops and the root ends. Peel the carrots, and cut off their tops.
• Simmer the vegetables carefully in a roomy pan with lightly salted water. They should be soft, but remain slightly hard in the middle.
• Combine the ingredients for the dressing.
• Place the vegetables in a bowl and drizzle the dressing over them while they're still warm. Serve the vegetables warm with the ham, butter, and bread.

MOULES VARIÉES

MUSSELS THREE WAYS

We should take a lesson from the French and eat more mussels. What a delicious and tasty quick food! What might scare you away is how you cook them. But relax. It's not difficult. Wash the mussels thoroughly and when they're done cooking, simply throw out the mussels that didn't open up.

BASIC RECIPE, 4 PEOPLE

1 net of blue mussels
2–4 shallots, depending on size
2 garlic cloves
2 tbsp extra virgin olive oil
black pepper and a bit of salt

· Wash and brush the mussels until they're clean. Tear off the "beard"— the stringy substance that is sometimes left along the edges. Throw out any mussels that are broken or already open and won't close when tapped. Place the mussels in a large bowl with cold water. This will help to remove any sand that might be left.
· Peel and mince the shallots and garlic. Heat the oil and sauté them for a few minutes; they should be bright but should not be browned. Season with pepper and a bit of salt.

Prepare everything up to here, and then continue by following one of the recipes on the next page.

MUSSELS THREE WAYS

MOULES MARINIÈRES WITH WHITE WINE AND THYME

Boil the mussels with white wine, shallots, garlic, and thyme and you'll have the French classic, *moules marinières*. What an amazing quick dish! The mussels are ready after 5 minutes. Fish them out and reduce the stock with cream if you'd like a creamier soup. Eat the mussels with a fork, and dip the bread in the delicious soup.

Basic recipe, see page 31
1 cup (250 ml) white wine
1 small sprig of thyme
½ cup (100 ml) whipping cream (optional)
baguette, for serving

· Follow the basic recipe and then add white wine to the mixture. Let the broth boil, then add the thyme and mussels. Stir well, and cover with the lid.
· Boil the mussels for about 5 minutes, until all the mussels have opened. Stir them, and throw away the ones that haven't opened.
· If you want, you can take out the mussels and add ½ cup (100 ml) of cream. Bring the stock to a boil with the cream, and allow it to simmer gently until it becomes a bit creamy. Then put the mussels in again.
· Serve the mussels with the broth and a baguette.

CIDER AND APPLES, NORMANDY STYLE

A unique, different way to serve mussels. Choose a tart apple. Boil the mussels in French cider, which is dry and has an acidic flavor. Top with finely chopped fresh apple and parsley.

Basic recipe, see page 31
1 cup (250 ml) dry cider
1 red apple
1 tbsp minced parsley
baguette, for serving

· Follow the basic recipe, then add cider to the mixture. Let the broth boil and add the mussels. Stir well and cover with a lid.
· Boil the mussels for about 5 minutes, until all the mussels have opened. Stir them, and throw away the ones that haven't opened.
· Core the apple and slice it into small, fine cubes. When the mussels are ready, mix in the apple and parsley.
· Serve with baguette.

CITRONETTE

I don't know how I'd manage without lemon in my cooking. Try this vinaigrette and serve it with freshly boiled mussels. Put a bowl of it on the table, and spoon it over the warm mussels.

Basic recipe, see page 31
1 cup (250 ml) white wine
baguette, for serving

CITRONETTE
1 organic lemon
1 shallot
4 tbsp extra virgin olive oil
1 pinch of salt
freshly ground black pepper

· Follow the basic recipe, then add the white wine to the mixture. Let the broth boil and add the mussels. Stir well and cover with a lid.
· Boil the mussels for about 5 minutes, until all the mussels have opened. Stir them, and throw away the ones that haven't opened.
· Wash the lemon and finely zest the peel. Squeeze out the juice. Peel and mince the shallot. Mix the lemon and shallot with the oil, salt, and pepper.
· Place the mussels in a dish and serve them with a baguette and with the citronette in a bowl on the side.

GRILLED BALTIC HERRING WITH LEMON AND PARSLEY

Have you ever tried grilling Baltic herring? You should! Because this dish is so delicious that you'll be astonished. It's important that the grill pan be hot enough that it smokes. The fish is first marinated with garlic and olive oil.

4 PEOPLE

1 lb (500 g) Baltic herring fillets
½ cup (100 ml) extra virgin olive oil
1 garlic clove
1 small flat-leaf parsley sprig
1 tsp salt
black pepper
1 tbsp canola oil, for pan-frying
lemon wedges and good bread, for serving

• Distribute the Baltic herring fillets in a dish. Pour the olive oil over them. Peel the garlic and mince it with the parsley. Pat into the groove of each Baltic herring fillet and mix so that the marinade covers all the fillets. Let the fish marinate for at least an hour in the fridge.

• Use a grill pan, if you have one, to grill the fish. If you don't have one, you can fry them in a regular frying pan. Heat up the grill pan—let it get really hot. It should smoke, but be careful! Brush the grilling surface with oil and season the fish with salt and pepper. Place the fish in the pan, skin-side down. Flip the fillets over once the edges get a light color to them, and finish frying them on the other side. Each side takes a few minutes. Squeeze lemon over the fillets and serve immediately with good bread.

ASPARAGUS WITH EGG AND LEMON

Sweet, soft asparagus is something I long for in the spring. Simmering it in lightly salted water and eating it with a creamy egg sauce . . . Delicious! Soft-boiled eggs seasoned with salt and pepper, along with lemon and olive oil, make a lovely sauce for the asparagus.

★ ★ ★ ★ ★

4 PEOPLE

1 bunch of white asparagus
4 eggs
sea salt and bread, for serving

DRESSING
1 lemon, juice
4 tbsp olive oil
1 tbsp finely chopped parsley
salt and freshly ground pepper

· Trim the asparagus and cut off an inch or two of the stalks.
· Boil the asparagus in lightly salted water for about 3–4 minutes. Test it with a sharp knife—the asparagus should have a raw center.
· Soft-boil the eggs, which should take about 4 minutes. Peel the eggs and mash them with a fork. Mix the ingredients for the dressing, and combine with the eggs.
· Place the asparagus in a dish and spoon over the egg sauce. Top with sea salt flakes and serve with bread.

SQUASH SOUP

Think of all the delicious things you can do with fresh squash, or courgette, as it is called in France. This soup, for example. The nutmeg adds a fine accent to the mild flavor of the squash, along with the chives.

4 PEOPLE

2¼ lb (1 kg) squash
2½ cups (600 ml) water
1 vegetable bouillon cube
½ cup (100 ml) cream
1½ tbsp (20 g) butter
salt and pepper
1 pinch of grated nutmeg
1 tbsp minced chives, for serving

· Cut off the tops and bottoms of the squash. Cut into slices about half an inch thick. Boil the water and bouillon cube, and add the squash. Allow to simmer for about 10 minutes, until the squash is soft.

· Mix into a smooth soup with an immersion blender, right in the pot.

· Dilute with water if the soup is too thick. Add cream and small cubes of butter. Bring the soup to a boil once more, and season it with salt, pepper, and nutmeg. Pour into individual bowls and garnish with chives.

SALAD WITH WARM GOAT CHEESE

Slices of baguette topped with goat cheese and olive oil—oven-baked to heavenly perfection. Make a salad with a fruity dressing and top it with the freshly baked cheese bread. That's even more delicious!

★ ★ ★ ★ ★

4 PEOPLE

4 slices of baguette
4 slices of chèvre (goat cheese)
extra virgin olive oil
1 head of lettuce, or baby greens

DRESSING
4 tbsp extra virgin olive oil
4 tbsp white balsamic vinegar
1 tsp honey
salt and freshly ground black pepper

· Set the oven to broil, 475°F (250°C). Place the bread on a baking sheet lined with parchment paper. Place a slice of chèvre on each piece of bread and drizzle with a tablespoon or two of olive oil. Broil at the top of the oven for about three minutes.
· Rinse the lettuce and dry it in a salad spinner, or carefully with a dish towel.
· Combine all of the ingredients for the dressing right in the salad bowl. Put in the lettuce and toss. Top with the warm goat cheese bread and serve immediately.

★ ★ ★ ★ ★

OPEN-FACED SANDWICH WITH HAM AND CHEESE

This is a really tasty open-faced sandwich, which comes out best if you use levain bread. The tartness of the sourdough bread really makes the sandwich. I'm lucky enough to live next to a French bakery—thanks, Benoit!

4 PEOPLE

∽ MONSIEUR ⌒

4 slices of levain bread
4 slices of ham, smoked or cooked
8 slices of cheese, e.g., Gruyère
4 tsp Dijon mustard
lettuce, for serving

BÉCHAMEL SAUCE
3½ tbsp (50 g) butter
1 tbsp wheat flour
¾ cup (200 ml) milk
1 tsp Dijon mustard
1 pinch finely grated nutmeg
salt and black pepper

• Place the bread on a baking sheet and place the sliced ham on top. Top with cheese—two slices per piece of bread—and spread the Dijon mustard evenly over top.
• Next, make the béchamel sauce. Melt the butter in a saucepan and add the flour. Whisk together and lightly brown the mixture for about one minute. This eliminates the taste of the flour. Slowly add the milk and whisk together into a smooth sauce. Season with mustard, nutmeg, and add salt and pepper to taste.
• Top each slice of bread with a tablespoon or two of the sauce. Bake at 450°F (225°C) for 8–10 minutes until the bread is golden-brown and the cheese has melted. Serve with lettuce.

∽ MADAME ⌒

• Same as above, but place a lightly fried egg on top of each sandwich. The egg should be fried on one side and have a creamy yolk.

OMELET WITH PORK BELLY, LETTUCE, AND CROUTONS

Here's a simplified variation of a French classic, topped with crisp pork belly, roasted croutons, lettuce, and a tangy vinaigrette. Eggs are good to keep at home—putting together an omelet isn't hard.

44

4 PEOPLE

OMELET
4 eggs
2 tbsp water
salt and a pinch of black pepper
1 tbsp butter
1 tbsp olive oil

ALONG WITH
2 oz (50 g) lightly salted
pork belly, or bacon
1 head of frisée lettuce,
or other crisp greens
4 slices sourdough bread
2 tbsp olive oil

VINAIGRETTE
4 tbsp olive oil
2 tbsp red wine vinegar
salt and pepper

• Start with the omelet: crack the eggs into a bowl and add the water. Whisk together and season with a touch of salt and pepper. Heat the butter and oil, and fry the omelet until lightly golden. Stir now and then with a fork until the omelet has set. Fold over and place on a dish.

• Slice the pork belly into cubes and fry until it is crispy. Allow it to drain on paper towels. Rinse the greens and cut into smaller pieces. Cube the bread and roast until crisp in a pan with oil.

• Mix together the vinaigrette. Top the omelet with the pork belly, lettuce, and croutons. Drizzle the dressing over the top.

POISSON À L'ANCHOÏADE

FISH WITH ANCHOVY SPREAD

Anchoïade is a delicious and savory southern French anchovy spread that's best for dipping raw vegetables in. You'll often get it with a glass of pastis before a meal. I serve this alongside fish with tomatoes and fennel.

4 PEOPLE

ANCHOÏADE
*1 tin of anchovies
5 pitted black olives
1 tbsp capers
1 garlic clove, minced
3 tbsp extra virgin olive oil
1 tbsp lemon juice
1 tsp red wine vinegar
black pepper*

*1 container of cherry tomatoes
3 tbsp olive oil
1 tsp sea salt*

*1 fennel
2 tbsp olive oil
salt*

*4 firm fish fillets (each 7 oz / 200 g), e.g., monkfish or other firm fish
4 tbsp olive oil
salt and black pepper
bread, for serving*

• Start with the *anchoïade*: place the anchovies in a bowl. Coarsely chop the olives and mix them with the anchovies. Add the capers and the garlic. Pour in the oil, lemon juice, and vinegar. Mix into a smooth sauce and season with freshly ground black pepper, to taste.
• Place the tomatoes in a baking dish and drizzle with a few tablespoons of oil. Sprinkle sea salt on top, and roast in the oven at 350°F (175°C) for about 30 minutes.
• Slice the fennel down the center and cut off the hard root at the very bottom. Cut into thin slices and roast quickly on high heat in a pan with olive oil. Salt it lightly and set aside.
• Rub the fish with the oil. Lightly salt and pepper it. Fry it for a couple minutes on each side, until both sides have a nice color. Don't fry it for too long, or it'll become rubbery and tough. Serve it with the *anchoïade*, bread, and the delicious vegetables.

SPRING SALAD

A simple, beautiful salad with different kinds of greens, radishes, and a delicious dressing. Excellent as a starter or alongside oven-grilled chicken.

4 PEOPLE

½ head of frisée lettuce
1 package mâche lettuce
½ bunch radishes

DRESSING
1 shallot
4 tbsp olive oil
4 tbsp red wine vinegar
salt and black pepper

· Rinse the greens and radishes. Cut it into coarse pieces and slice the radishes thinly.
· Prepare the dressing right in the salad bowl: peel and mince the shallot, then mix it with the oil, vinegar, salt, and pepper. Toss the greens in the dressing. Serve immediately.

ARTICHOKES WITH VINAIGRETTE

My youngest daughter, Siri, loves artichokes with vinaigrette. So do I! It's a lovely way to share a meal. Pull warm leaves from a freshly cooked artichoke and dip them in a tart dressing. Finally, you reach the tufts of white "hair" and underneath, the tasty artichoke heart. Pick off the threads and cut the bottom into pieces. Place it in the dressing. You'll be fighting amongst yourselves for the last few pieces.

4 PEOPLE

4 artichokes
1 tsp salt

VINAIGRETTE
1 lemon
4 tbsp white wine vinegar
¼ cup (50 ml) extra virgin olive oil
salt and freshly ground black pepper

· Cut off the artichoke stalks, so that they can sit flat. Boil water and salt in a large pot. Simmer the artichokes until tender, for about 30–40 minutes.
· Prepare the dressing: Slice the lemon and squeeze out the juice. Mix the juice in a bowl with the vinegar and oil. Add salt and pepper to taste.
· Serve the artichokes on individual plates. Work your way down to the artichoke heart, pulling off one leaf at a time, dipping it in the vinaigrette, and pulling off the meat with your teeth. Pick away the the small threads and slice the bottom into pieces and eat it with the vinaigrette.

OMELET WITH CHEESE AND HERBS

It's not hard to whip up an omelet. But don't fry it for too long. It should stay creamy in the center. Fill it with soft fresh cheese and Gruyère, which has a nutty flavor. Together with mixed fresh herbs—fines herbes—it flavors the omelet and makes it unbelievably delicious.

★ ★ ★ ★ ★

2 PEOPLE

4 eggs
4 tbsp cold water
¼ cup (50 ml) finely chopped fresh herbs:
parsley, thyme, tarragon, and chives
salt and black pepper
1 tbsp butter
1 tbsp oil
2 oz (50 g) finely grated Gruyère
1 boursin cheese (or any type of soft,
creamy cheese)
3 tbsp crème fraîche or sour cream
bread, for serving

Crack the eggs into a bowl and whisk them together with the water. Add in half of the chopped herbs and season with salt and pepper.

Heat the butter and oil in a frying pan. Pour in the omelet batter and fry over low heat for a few minutes. Stir carefully a few times, so the omelet cooks completely. Fry the omelet until the edges begin to stiffen and get a bit of color underneath. Don't fry it too long; it should still be creamy in the middle. Spread the grated cheese over top. Mash the boursin and crème fraîche together, then dollop onto the center of the omelet. Fold the sides in toward the middle. Top with the rest of the herbs and serve with bread.

TOMATO AND ORANGE SALAD

★ ★ ★ ★ ★

Here, the flavors of southern France are combined with North African influences. It tastes of acidity and a touch of sharpness against the saltiness of olives.

4 PEOPLE

3 large tomatoes
2 oranges
1 red onion
10–12 high quality black olives with pits

VINAIGRETTE

1 tbsp finely chopped tarragon
1 tbsp finely chopped parsley
2 tbsp red wine vinegar
4 tbsp extra virgin olive oil
salt and freshly ground black pepper

· Slice the tomatoes into thin discs. Peel the oranges with a sharp knife and cut them into thin slices. Peel and slice the onion the same way.

· Mix all the ingredients for the dressing in a bowl: herbs, vinegar, oil, salt, and pepper.

· Arrange the tomatoes, the oranges, and the onion on a dish and drizzle the dressing over top. Decorate with olives. This salad makes for a piquant starter, and is delicious alongside grilled lamb or chicken.

PAIN BAGNA

STREET SANDWICH WITH TUNA AND VEGETABLES

Delightful street food: an all-in-one sandwich. When Mom and I were in Nice, we bought pain bagna from a stall near the beach—hollowed-out white rolls filled with a salad of tuna, vegetables, and olives. A dressing with Dijon mustard adds a bold, delicious flavor to the whole sandwich. Quite simply, it's a whole meal on a roll.

★★★★★

4 PEOPLE

4 hearty white rolls
1 can tuna
2 tomatoes
¼ cucumber
½ red onion
4 anchovies
½ cup (100 ml) black olives
2 boiled eggs, in wedges

VINAIGRETTE

2 tbsp white wine vinegar
4 tbsp extra virgin olive oil
1 tsp Dijon mustard
1 tsp French herbs or thyme
salt and freshly ground black pepper

· Slice off the top of each roll and scoop out a bit of the bread beneath. Drain the tuna and mash it with a fork on a plate. Cut the tomato into thin slices. If they're too big, cut them in half. Peel and core the cucumber, then cut it into small cubes. Thinly slice the red onion.
· Fill the rolls with the tuna, tomato slices, cucumber, and onion. Top with the anchovies, olives, and egg.
· Whisk together the ingredients for the vinaigrette in a bowl. Season with salt and pepper to taste. Pour a tablespoon or two of the vinaigrette over the sandwich filling and replace the tops of the rolls. If you have time, allow the sandwiches to sit for a while and soak up the flavors. Rosé wine pairs excellently with this!

★ AU FOUR ★

FROM THE OVEN

The oven really deserves to be used more, as that's where temperatures stay evenly warm. If you put in a beef stew to simmer on low heat, you can be certain it will come out just right. The meat becomes juicier, and you can go on to do something else while the stew takes care of itself. Vegetables, too, take on a pleasant flavor when baked in the oven. They come out sweeter and more delicious, and they have a fuller aroma.

POULET RÔTI AU CITRON

LEMON-ROASTED WHOLE CHICKEN

The savior of fridays in my home and one of those dishes that's as delicious as delicious can be. The secret to my chicken is that I cook it for a long time at a low temperature—that makes it juicier than you could ever imagine. Together with garlic and lemon, it gets an extra kick of flavor.

4 people

1 fresh chicken
1 organic lemon
4 garlic cloves
1 bunch of fresh thyme
2 tbsp olive oil
salt and freshly ground black pepper
oven-baked potatoes or bread and salad, for serving

➤ Preheat the oven to 300°F (150°C). Place the chicken in a baking dish. Slice the lemon and squeeze the juice out over the chicken; then place the two halves of the lemon inside the chicken itself.

➤ Crush the garlic cloves lightly with the flat of the blade of your knife; there's no need to peel them. Push these inside the chicken too, along with a handful of thyme.

➤ Pour the oil over the chicken and season it with salt and pepper. Place the chicken in the middle of the oven and cook for about 2 hours, until the juices run clear when you pierce the thigh of the chicken with a sharp knife.

➤ Oven-baked potatoes or bread and salad are great on the side.

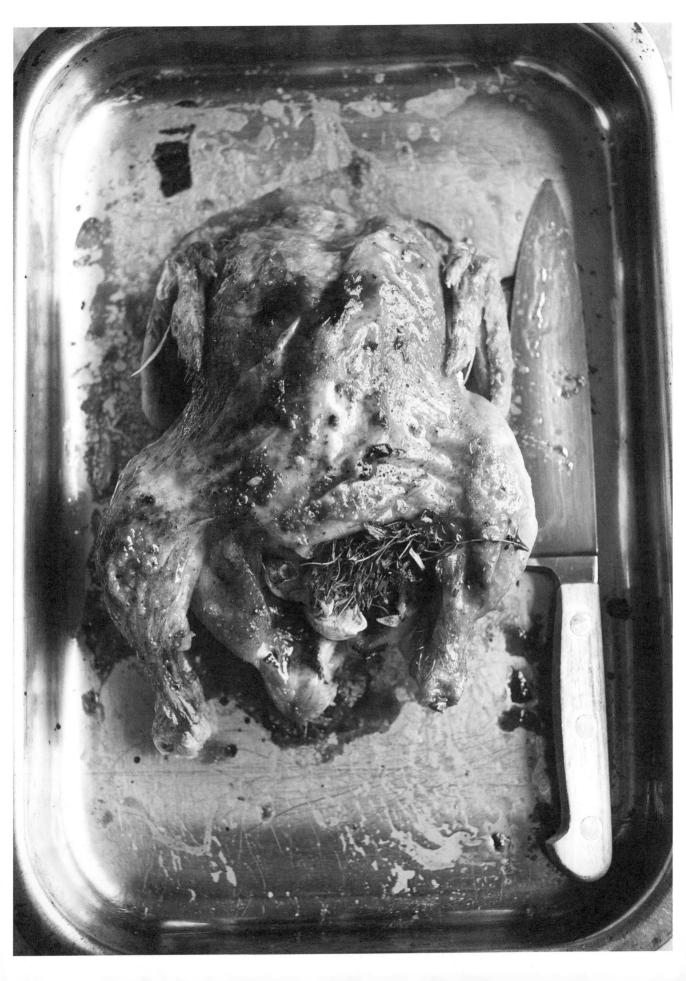

TIAN À LA COURGE

OVEN-BAKED OMELET WITH SQUASH

An oven-baked omelet filled with vegetables is called a tian in Provence. I like to stuff mine with baked butternut squash, which is sweet and tasty. Different vegetables, herbs, onion, and aged cheese give it a good flavor and make for a filling dish alongside salad and bread. I usually serve it cold or warm because it tastes much better that way.

4 people

½ small butternut squash
olive oil
1 squash
1 yellow onion
2 garlic cloves
salt and freshly ground black pepper
1 tsp french herbs, Herbes de Provence
5 eggs
½ cup (100 ml) grated Parmesan or Gruyère
1 pinch sea salt
salad, for serving

⟶ Preheat the oven to 400°F (200°C). Peel the butternut squash and slice it into smaller pieces. Place it in a baking dish and sprinkle a tablespoon or two of oil over top. Cook it in the oven until it is soft and takes on a brownish color, about 20 minutes.

⟶ Cut the squash into slices. Peel and mince the onion and garlic. Heat oil in a pan and sauté the squash, onion, and garlic for a few minutes. Season with salt and pepper. Add the herbs near the end and stir.

⟶ Whisk together the eggs and cheese with a pinch of sea salt. Layer the butternut squash and other vegetables in a baking pan with removable sides or in an oven-safe frying pan. Pour on the egg and cheese mixture and bake at 350°F (175°C) in the middle of the oven for about 40 minutes. Serve warm with salad.

OVEN-BAKED VEGETABLES, PROVENCE-STYLE

If you ask me, vegetables baked in the oven come out so much tastier. My ratatouille gratin is delicious on its own, or served with oven-baked chicken. It's also wonderful with grilled lamb or a lamb roast stuffed with garlic and rubbed with herbs and olive oil.

4 people

1 squash
1 eggplant
4 tomatoes
1–2 red bell peppers
1 red onion
1 garlic clove
¼ cup (50 ml) olive oil
1 tbsp Herbes de Provence
1 tsp sea salt
a pinch of black pepper
½ cup (100 ml) grated gruyère
2 tbsp breadcrumbs

➤ Preheat the oven to 400°F (200°C). Rinse and slice the squash, eggplant, and tomatoes. Slice the bell pepper into pieces. Peel and slice the red onion. Layer the vegetables in a baking dish.
➤ Peel and mince the garlic, then blend with oil, herbs, salt, and pepper. Sprinkle the mixture over the vegetables in the pan. Top it with the grated cheese and breadcrumbs. Bake in the oven for about 30 minutes until the vegetables have taken on a nice color.

LILIANE'S OVEN-BAKED TOMATOES

A friend invited me to her home for dinner in Paris and his mother made these delicious tomatoes. Large tomatoes are hollowed out and filled with a ground meat mixture that's seasoned with herbs and garlic. They're baked in the oven and served with rice.

4 people

4 large tomatoes, on the vine
7 oz (200 g) ground beef and pork
2 garlic cloves, minced
1 tbsp minced parsley
1 tbsp minced rosemary
1 tsp lemon zest
3½ oz (100 g) finely grated Parmesan cheese
1 egg yolk
olive oil
salt and pepper
rice, for serving

➤ Cut off the tops of the tomatoes, so they're like lids. Scoop out the insides with a spoon.
➤ Place the ground meat in a bowl and add the garlic, herbs, lemon zest, Parmesan cheese, egg yolk, a bit of oil, salt, and pepper. Stir into a smooth mixture.
➤ Fill the tomatoes up just until the meat mixture sticks out of the top. Place them in an oven-safe dish. Replace the tops of the tomatoes and drizzle oil on top. Bake for about an hour at 350°F (175°C). Serve with rice.

PAUPIETTE
18.00 €/Kg

FARCE
à T...

TOMATE
FARCIE
8.80 €/Kg

PIE WITH LEEK AND PORK BELLY

This pie is a dear old friend of mine. I must have made at least a hundred of these throughout the years. Simple yet genius, with the crispy smoked pork that meets a creamy filling of eggs, leeks, and aged cheese, top with delicious, sweet tomatoes and fresh herbs.

6 people

Crust:
7 tbsp (100 g) butter
1 cup (250 ml) wheat flour
1 pinch sea salt
2–3 tbsp ice cold water

Filling:
1 leek
1 tbsp butter
5 oz (150 g) smoked lean pork belly
5 oz (150 g) gruyère cheese
4 eggs
1¾ cup (400 ml) cream
salt and black pepper
mixed cherry tomatoes, fresh basil, and thyme, for garnishing

☞ Start with the crust: slice the cold butter into small cubes. Place them in a bowl with the flour and salt, and quickly mix them together to make a grainy mixture. Add the water, and form into a smooth dough. Cover with plastic wrap and place in the fridge for about 30 minutes.

☞ Preheat the oven to 400°F (200°C). Roll out the dough and press it into a pie dish. Prick the bottom with a fork and pre-bake the crust for about 10 minutes.

☞ Slice the leeks lengthwise and rinse them thoroughly in cold water. Shred them finely and fry them lightly in butter, being careful not to let them become too brown. Cut away the rind from the pork belly. Dice the pork finely and fry it until crispy, then place it on paper towels to cool. Coarsely grate the cheese and fill the pie shell with the leeks, pork belly, and cheese.

☞ Whisk together the eggs and cream. Season with a bit of salt and pepper. Pour the mixture into the crust and bake in the middle of the oven for about 30–40 minutes, until the pie is a nice golden brown.

☞ Slice the tomatoes into small pieces and top the pie with the tomatoes, fresh basil, and thyme.

TOMATO SALAD WITH OVEN-BAKED EGGPLANT AND FETA CHEESE

It's fun to surprise your taste buds with different tastes and textures. like the ones in this salad.
The eggplant is baked in the oven before being turned into a juicy mash: once on the plate.
the eggplant enjoys the company of juicy sun-ripened tomatoes. feta cheese. and aromatic basil.

★ 4 PEOPLE ★

1 eggplant
2 tbsp olive oil
4 tomatoes
3½ oz (100 g) feta cheese
1 bunch fresh basil

Vinaigrette:
2 tbsp red wine vinegar
4 tbsp extra virgin olive oil
salt and black pepper

➤ Preheat the oven to 400°F (200°C). Cut the eggplant into slices, discarding the top and bottom. Place the slices on a baking sheet. Drizzle with olive oil and bake in the oven for about 15–20 minutes until golden and tender. Place the slices on a plate and mash them lightly with a fork. Let the eggplant mash cool down.
➤ Slice the tomatoes. Mash the cheese with a fork on a small plate. Mix the ingredients for the dressing.
➤ Place the tomatoes on a serving dish and distribute the mashed eggplant and feta cheese on top. Sprinkle the dressing over the tomatoes and garnish with basil.

OVEN-BAKED PORK ROAST

The loin is a lovely cut of meat that becomes deliciously juicy when it's baked in the oven. Be generous with the salt and black pepper. and sear the roast all the way around. Pour a tasty mixture of wine and herbs on top and bake the roast in the oven. Read a book and have a glass of something nice. Voilà! Dinner is served!

★ 4 PEOPLE ★

1¼ lb (600 g) boneless pork loin
½ cup (100 ml) white wine
3 garlic cloves
1 bay leaf
1 tbsp minced thyme
2 tbsp olive oil
salt and freshly ground black pepper
1 tbsp butter
salad and flavorful bread, for serving

➤ Let the meat sit out until it's at room temperature. Preheat the oven to 300°F (150°C). Pour the wine into a bowl. Peel the garlic and place in the wine, whole, along with the bay leaf, thyme, and oil. Season the roast evenly with salt and pepper.
➤ Heat the butter in a pan. Sear the meat all around, so it gets a nicely browned exterior. Place it in a baking dish and pour the wine mixture over it. Rinse the pan with a few tablespoons of water and pour that over the roast, too. Place the roast in the oven and cook for about an hour and a half.
➤ Let the meat cool a bit and slice it thinly. It's a great idea to cook small whole potatoes in the oven at the same time, too. In that case, place the potatoes in the oven during the last 30–45 minutes of the roast's cooking time, and drizzle with olive oil. Serve with the jus, salad, and a tasty bread.

ONION PIE WITH ANCHOVIES AND OLIVES

I'm giving you a heads up: once you start eating this pie, you won't be able to stop! The bottom is a buttery pie dough that's rolled thinly and filled with sautéed onions, anchovies, and olives. I tried this wonderful pie for the first time at a bakery in Nice. It's called pissaladière, and you can often buy slices of it in French bakeries. I call it Nizzapizza.

6–8 people

Pie dough
7 oz (200 g) butter, straight from the fridge
1 egg yolk
2½ cups (600 ml) wheat flour
salt

Topping
3 yellow onions
3 red onions
olive oil
1 tin anchovies
8–10 black olives with pits
1 tsp thyme or rosemary, optional
1 egg yolk, for brushing

☞ Start by making the dough: Slice the butter into small cubes. Place them in a bowl with the egg yolk and the flour. Add salt and work quickly into a smooth dough. Let it rest for 30 minutes in the fridge.

☞ Peel and slice the onions thinly. Sauté until transparent in a decently sized pan with oil. Make sure they don't brown. Place the onions in a colander and press out any extra liquid.

☞ Roll out the dough into a rectangle of about 10 x 12 inches (25 x 30 cm) on a floured surface. Transfer it to a baking sheet and fold the sides into a crust all around the edges.

☞ Top with the onions, anchovies, and olives, distributing them evenly. If you'd like, you can scatter some thyme or rosemary on top. Brush the edges with a beaten egg yolk and bake in the middle of the oven for about 20 minutes at 350°F (175°C).

★ BŒUF BOURGUIGNON ★

RICH BEEF STEW

A juicy and flavorful stew with chuck steak, onions, and generous amounts of red wine. Try simmering the stew at a low temperature in the oven. Easy to do, and the stew takes care of itself. It's even more delicious if you make it one day in advance.

★ 4–6 PEOPLE ★

1 lb (500 g) chuck steak
1 tsp salt
black pepper
1 tbsp butter + 1 tbsp olive oil
2 tbsp wheat flour
½ cup (100 ml) water
5 oz (150 g) smoked pork belly
2 garlic cloves
1 yellow onion
3 carrots
1 bottle of fruity red wine
¼ cup (50 ml) veal or beef stock
1 tbsp tomato purée
1 bay leaf
1 bunch of thyme
10 pearl onions
7 oz (200 g) mushrooms
1 tbsp butter
½ cup (100 ml) minced parsley
bread, for serving

↪ Preheat the oven to 350°F (175°C). Slice the meat into large chunks and season with salt and pepper. Heat the butter and oil in a pan and brown the meat on all sides. Sprinkle the flour on top and cook for another minute or two. Place the meat in an oven-safe dish. Rinse the pan with the water and pour it over the meat, too.

↪ Slice the pork belly into small cubes and brown it lightly in the pan. Take it out and allow it to drain on paper towels. Peel the garlic, onion, and carrots, then coarsely chop the onion and carrots. Brown the vegetables in the fat from the pork belly. Place the vegetables and pork in the dish. Add the wine, veal stock, tomato purée, and herbs.

↪ Cover the dish and cook the stew in the middle of the oven for about 3 hours, until the meat is really good and dark.

↪ While you're waiting, peel the pearl onions and rinse the mushrooms. Slice the mushrooms in half. Heat butter in a pan. Start by lightly browning the onions, then remove them and set them aside. Do the same with the mushrooms. When the stew has cooked for two hours, add the onions and mushrooms. Let the stew simmer for another hour, or until the meat begins to fall apart. Garnish with chopped parsley and serve with bread.

73

DE CAMPAGNE

★★★★★

RUSTIC

What's fun about rustic, country-style food is that it's always a meal that's good to share: soups that have been slow-simmered to juicy perfection, stews with red meat or chicken. Food for everyone! Find yourself a sturdy, hefty dish that's oven-safe and pretty enough to be the centerpiece on your table. Invite friends over and socialize over a well-cooked meal. You may find you'll linger for hours.

Bouquet garni is a bouquet of herbs tied up with cooking twine, used to add flavor and aroma to any dish. Simply place it in the pot with whatever is cooking, and fish it out when the food's ready!

VEGETABLES IN BROTH WITH SPICES AND WHITE WINE

À la grecque means that you cook the vegetables in a flavorful broth with herbs and good oil. When the vegetables are ready, you cook down the broth and pour it over as a marinade. They'll last for several days in the fridge, and are perfect to serve as part of a buffet. The spice ras el hanout is a popular Arab spice that gives the vegetables both a piquant flavor and a beautiful color.

A bouquet garni is a bundle of various herbs. You can use a few sprigs of thyme, parsley, bay leaves, celery stalks, and leeks. Everything gets packed together into a bundle, and tied together with cooking twine. Then, the bundle is cooked to add flavor and aroma. When the food's ready, simply fish out the small herb bundle, which has now served its purpose!

★ ★ ★ ★ ★

4–6 PEOPLE

2 baby leeks
1 lb (500 g) fresh mushrooms
1 small head of cauliflower

COURT BOUILLON
2 shallots
1 tbsp olive oil
1 tsp coriander seeds
1 tsp ras el hanout (or ½ tsp turmeric)
½ cup (100 ml) water
¾ cup (200 ml) dry white wine
3 tbsp extra virgin olive oil
½ organic lemon, zest and juice
2 tbsp white wine vinegar
1 bouquet garni (herb bouquet: tie pars-ley, celery, and thyme together with cooking twine)
6 whole black peppercorns

ON THE SIDE
Bread, and preferably charcuterie (e.g., paté or ham)

• Cut off the root and a bit of the tops of the leeks. Cut them lengthwise and rinse them thoroughly. Slice them into pieces about 6 inches (15 cm) long. Rinse the mushrooms and slice larger ones into halves or quarters. Rinse and divide the cauliflower into smaller pieces.

• Peel and mince the shallot. Sauté it in olive oil in a saucepan for a few minutes. Make sure it doesn't brown. Add the coriander seeds and ras el hanout or turmeric. Stir and add water, wine, and oil. Finish with the fresh lemon juice and finely grated lemon zest, vinegar, bouquet garni, and black peppercorns.

• Bring the mixture to a boil, then add all the vegetables. Simmer them until tender, for about 5 minutes. Place them in thoroughly cleaned glass jars and fill them about halfway. Reduce the broth for about 5 minutes, without a lid. Pour it over the vegetables and seal the jars.

• Serve the vegetables at room temperature, or cold, with bread, preferably alongside charcuterie (e.g., paté or ham).

VEGETABLE SOUP WITH BASIL PASTE

If you use broad beans, remember to hull them—that is, take them out of their pods. The white membrane around each bean usually needs to be removed too, unless it's the very beginning of the broad bean season. A paste made of basil, garlic, and oil is called pistou in Provence and makes this soup taste the best!

4 PEOPLE

1 potato
2 tomatoes
the white portion of 1 leek
1 celery stalk
3½ oz (100 g) small dried white beans, soaked overnight
salt and pepper
1 squash
3½ oz (100 g) green beans, (haricots verts)
3½ oz (100 g) snow peas or broad beans

PISTOU

2 garlic cloves
1 bunch fresh basil
3½ oz (100 g) gruyère or Parmesan cheese
3½ tbsp (50 ml) olive oil
freshly ground black pepper

· Peel and slice the potato. Cut the tomatoes into smaller pieces. Thinly slice the leeks and finely chop the celery stalk.

· Boil 1 quart (1 liter) of water in a saucepan. Add the potato, tomatoes, leeks, celery, and white beans. Season with salt and pepper and cook over low heat for about 30 minutes.

· Cut the squash into slices and place it, the haricots verts, and the snow peas in the pan. Cook for 10 more minutes.

· Mince the garlic and basil. Shred the cheese and blend it with the olive oil and with the minced garlic and basil. If you have one, use a mortar and pestle to grind the mixture for a short while. Season with pepper. Serve the soup piping hot with the pistou.

ONION SOUP

This is a clear soup with tons of onions and herbs, seasoned with white wine. On top are crispy slices of sourdough bread, baked in the oven with aged cheese. A classic soup on the French bistro menu. The flavor should be round and rich!

★ ★ ★ ★ ★

4 PEOPLE

6 yellow onions
2 garlic cloves
1 leek
2 tbsp butter
2 tbsp olive oil
1 tbsp wheat flour
¾ cup (200 ml) white wine
4 ¼ cups (1 liter) vegetable
or chicken stock
1 tbsp minced fresh thyme
1 bay leaf
sea salt and freshly
ground black pepper
4 slices of sourdough bread
2 oz (50 g) grated aged cheese,
e.g., comté or gruyère

· Peel the onion and garlic. Slit the leek lengthwise and rinse it thoroughly. Slice the onion and leek thinly, and mince the garlic.

· Heat the butter and oil in a large pan. Sauté the onion until it's transparent, but not brown. Add the garlic when the onion is almost done. Dust with the flour and allow it to cook for another minute or two.

· Pour in the wine, stock, thyme, and bay leaf. Then stir to dissolve the flour. Cook for about 30 minutes. Season with salt and pepper to taste.

· Preheat the oven to 450°F (225°C). Pour the soup into individual oven-safe bowls. Place in a deep dish. Top the soup with a slice of bread and distribute the cheese on top. Bake for about 5 minutes, until the cheese is melted.

CHICKEN STEW WITH CLEAR BROTH AND VEGETABLES

A classic French stew that's great to share. Most often, it contains beef brisket, sausages, vegetables, and chicken. Here, I've simplified the stew so it'll be quicker to make. When I invited my friend François and his friend over, his friend exclaimed: "Mon dieu—that was even better than my wife's!"

4–6 PEOPLE

6 ⅓ cups (1 ½ liters) water + 1 tsp salt
1 chicken
1 tbsp olive oil
salt and black pepper
1 net pearl onions
3 garlic cloves
1 tsp whole white peppercorns
3 potatoes
2 parsnips
½ rutabaga, approx. ⅔ lb (300 g)
4 carrots
½ leek
2 stalks celery leaves
Dijon mustard and bread, for serving

SPICE BOUQUET

2 bay leaves
1 small sprig fresh thyme
1 small sprig parsley
cooking twine

• Use a decently sized saucepan. Boil the water with salt. Cut the chicken into eight pieces. Heat the oil in a pan. Season the chicken with salt and pepper. Brown it lightly in the pan. Then move it to the saucepan. Boil and skim off the top of the water. Turn down the heat and place the lid on top.

• Peel the onion and garlic. Place them in the stew whole, along with the white peppercorns.

• Peel the potato, parsnips, rutabaga, and carrots. Slice them into smaller pieces and place them in the stew along with the leek and celery, which should also be cut into small pieces.

• Tie together the spice bouquet with the cooking twine and add it in as well. Simmer the stew, covered, for about 40 minutes, until the chicken is ready. Serve with Dijon mustard and bread.

FISH SOUP WITH SAFFRON, TOMATO, AND RED PEPPER AIOLI

This one's a clear fish soup I tried for the first time in Aix-en-Provence. I was startled when a plate of clear soup came in with bread, grated cheese, and rust-red aioli in a bowl. Where's the fish? But that's how soupe de poisson is served. Different types of fish and vegetables are cooked into a flavorful broth with spices, and then strained. I make my soupe de poisson with pieces of fish in it. The paste that goes with it is a sort of mayonnaise flavored with roasted red pepper, chili, and saffron. Flavor fireworks are guaranteed!

---

4 PEOPLE

1 yellow onion
1 leek
1 fennel
1 celery stalk
2 garlic cloves
4 tomatoes
4 tbsp extra virgin olive oil
1 pinch whole fennel seeds
1 pinch chili flakes or
cayenne pepper
1 pinch of saffron
1 tbsp tomato purée
¾ cup (200 ml) good fish stock
4¼ cups (1 liter) water
1 lb (500 g) white fish fillet
(e.g., cod, walleye, or
haddock)
3½ oz (100 g) gruyère cheese
1 baguette

ROUILLE

1 red bell pepper
2 garlic cloves
1 spicy chili pepper
2 egg yolks
½ cup (100 ml) extra
virgin olive oil
½ lemon
1 pinch saffron
salt and freshly ground
black pepper

• Peel and coarsely chop the onion. Slit the leek lengthwise and rinse it in cold water. Slice it into thin strips. Cut the fennel down the center and cut away the root stalk at the bottom. Shred the fennel and celery stalk. Peel and mince the garlic. Dice the tomatoes coarsely.

• Heat the oil in a saucepan. Place the onion in first, and allow it to sweat a bit without browning. Then add the rest of the vegetables and cook on low heat for about 5 minutes, again without browning. Season with fennel, chili, saffron, and tomato purée, sauté for another minute or two, then pour in the stock and water. Simmer with the lid on for 30 minutes.

• While you wait, prepare the rouille: grill the red pepper whole at 440°F (225°C) in the oven for about 20 minutes, until it develops black bubbles on its surface. Take it out and let it cook for a bit. Cut it down the middle and remove the stem and seeds. Remove its skin with a sharp knife. Slice the pepper into smaller pieces. Peel the garlic and mince it with the chili pepper. Place the red pepper, garlic, and chili pepper in a food processor and process it into a smooth paste.

• Put the egg yolks in a bowl and add the oil, a bit at a time. Whisk into a fluffy mayonnaise. Mix in the red pepper paste along with the fresh lemon juice and saffron. Combine thoroughly, and season with salt and pepper to taste.

• Continue with the soup: strain the delicious broth, and press the vegetables with a wooden spoon to get as much liquid out of them as possible. Toss the vegetables, and boil the broth again. Slice the fish into small portion-sized pieces and place it in the soup. Simmer for about 3 minutes and set aside.

• Finely grate the cheese and slice the bread thinly. Roast the slices of bread in the middle of the oven at 400°F (200°C) for about 5 minutes, or until they're slightly browned. Serve the soup in individual bowls with slices of bread topped with the rouille and grated cheese, which can be melted in the soup.

NAVARIN DE PRINTEMPS

SPRINGTIME LAMB STEW

Navarin de printemps is actually a French lamb stew with young vegetables that taste like spring and the beginning of summer. But I'm incredibly fond of veal, so I make my stew with it instead. Do whatever you like! If you like lamb, use it, by all means. This stew really has got it all: tender meat, tasty vegetables, and a delightful broth.

4 PEOPLE

4 pieces veal or lamb, 7 oz (200 g) each
1 tbsp wheat flour
salt and freshly ground white pepper
2 tbsp butter
1 tbsp olive oil
1 bouquet garni (tie a few stalks of
parsley, thyme, and a bay leaf
together with cooking twine)
1 leek
2 yellow onions
1 garlic clove
¾ cups (200 ml) white wine
2 tomatoes
1 bunch fresh onions
½ bunch carrots
3½ oz (100 g) snow peas or haricots
verts
2 tbsp wheat flour
1 tbsp butter
½ cup (100 ml) cream
salt and freshly ground white pepper
boiled potatoes or bread, for serving

· Cut the meat into smaller pieces, coat them in flour, and season with salt and pepper on both sides. Heat the butter and oil in a large saucepan and brown both sides of the meat.

· Tie together a bouquet garni.

· Slit the leek lengthwise and rinse it thoroughly in cold water. Shred it finely. Peel and mince the onions and garlic. Remove the meat, place it off to the side, and put the leek, onions, and garlic in the saucepan. Sauté for a few minutes without browning them.

· Pour the wine on top and put the meat in. Simmer for at least an hour, until the meat is tender. Remove the seeds from the tomato and cut it into strips. Slice the fresh onions into small pieces. Peel the carrots and cut them into small pieces, too. Place the tomatoes, onions, and carrots into the stew. Simmer them until they're tender. Add in the snow peas.

· Mix the flour and butter in a dish with a fork. Stir this mixture into the stew and boil it, adding the cream. Season with salt and pepper to taste.

· Serve with boiled potatoes or bread.

VINEGAR CHICKEN

This is yet another really delicious chicken recipe. You don't need to have very much on hand to put this stew together. Buy a nice, fresh chicken and sear it in butter. Then simmer it with herbs and vinegar. You'll love it!

4 PEOPLE

1 fresh chicken
1 whole head of fresh garlic
1 tbsp butter
1 tbsp minced fresh thyme
½ cup (100 ml) red wine vinegar
1 bay leaf
cooked vegetables and bread, for serving

• Cut the chicken into four pieces. Lightly crush the garlic with the end of a knife. If you can't find fresh garlic, use three cloves of regular garlic and do the same.
• Heat the butter, covered, in a pan. Sauté the garlic with its skin for a few minutes, without letting it brown. Add the chicken and sear it lightly on both sides. Season with thyme, salt, and pepper. Pour over the vinegar, add the bay leaf, and cover.
• Let the chicken simmer while covered for about 30–40 minutes, until the juice runs clear when you prick the thigh with a knife. Serve with cooked vegetables and good bread.

CHICKEN STEW WITH APPLE CIDER AND CREAM

Chicken stews are always tasty. Here I've prepared a popular stew, flavored with onions, pork belly, cream, and apple cider. The flavors are rich and borrowed from Normandy, where they make exquisitely dry, fresh apple cider.

4 PEOPLE

1 chicken
2 tbsp wheat flour
salt and freshly ground black pepper
2 tbsp butter
3½ oz (100 g) lightly salted pork belly
10 pearl onions
1¼ cups (300 ml) dry apple cider
1 bouquet garni (tie together a few sprigs of parsley, thyme,
and a bay leaf with cooking twine)
½ cup (100 ml) cream
1 tbsp parsley
salad and bread, for serving

- Divide the chicken into eight pieces. Flour, salt, and pepper each piece. Sear them in a pan with half of the butter, so the chicken gets a nice color all around. Transfer the chicken to a large pot.
- Slice the pork belly into small cubes and sauté it in the pan in the remaining butter. Peel the onions and add them to the pan when the pork begins to take on some color and become crispy. Continue sautéing until the onion, too, has browned. Then place the onions and pork in the pot with the chicken—use a slotted spoon to avoid picking up too much of the fat. Pour in the cider and bring to a boil, without covering.
- Tie together the parsley, thyme, and bay leaf to make a small bouquet garni. Place it in the bottom of the pot and cover. Simmer for about 30 minutes. Add the cream and cook, uncovered, for about 10 more minutes, then garnish with parsley. Serve with salad and rustic sourdough bread.

UN BON MARIAGE
A MARRIAGE OF FLAVORS

In France, people have a very unique sense of which ingredients work best together. How they should be prepared, when they're in season, and when they taste the best. When the ingredients and execution are perfectly composed, the result is a marriage that brings happiness—your stomach will be happy, and so will you. Add in a few good drinks that go well with the food, and you'll have a marriage of flavors on every level. It might sound pretentious, but fresh sole with a buttery sauce is, quite simply, peerlessly delicious French food. This is, after all, about exquisitely delicious food!

SOLE WITH BUTTER SAUCE AND BUTTER-FRIED CAPERS

I love fish, and the creamy butter sauce beurre blanc is heavenly with flavorful flatfish like sole or witch flounder. My take on it involves adding butter-fried capers with lemon, which adds extra acidity and delicious crispiness to the fish. Keep in mind that the sauce should be served immediately after making it: if it warms up, it'll melt away.

★ SEE PICTURE ON PAGE 93 ★

4 people

1 sole, 2½– 3½ lbs (1– 1½ kg), or four smaller witch flounder
1 tbsp wheat flour
2 tbsp butter
salt
½ lemon, zest and juice
2 tbsp butter
2 tbsp capers
1 tbsp minced parsley
baguette, for serving

Beurre blanc
4 tbsp white wine vinegar
½ cup (100 ml) dry white wine
4 minced shallots
salt and white pepper
7 oz (200 g) butter
1 tbsp lemon juice
salt and black pepper

→ Start by making the beurre blanc: Pour the vinegar and wine into a saucepan. Add the shallots, salt, and pepper. Boil, uncovered, until about two tablespoons of liquid remain. Add the butter, cut into small cubes, and whisk vigorously to make a smooth sauce. Season with lemon juice, salt, and pepper, and set aside.

→ Rinse the fish and scale it. This is easiest with a scrubbing sponge; use the green surface and lightly scrub the darker side of the fish, or scrape it with a sharp knife. Finish by rinsing it in cold water. Cut off the head, and trim the sides. You can also ask a fishmonger to do this—but leave the white skin on, as that's where much of the flavor is. Dry off the fish with paper towels.

→ Coat both sides of the fish in flour, and heat the butter. Salt the fish and fry it until golden-brown on both sides. Zest the lemon and squeeze its juice into a bowl. Brown the butter; when it's hazelnut brown, add the capers. Stir, then mix with the lemon zest, lemon juice, and parsley. Drizzle the caper butter over the fish and serve the beurre blanc in a bowl on the side. Enjoy with baguette and a good white wine.

WARM GOAT CHEESE SALAD WITH APPLE

Goat cheese is available in many different varieties in French cheese shops. Choose one with a flavor that isn't too sharp.

4 people

7 oz (200 g) goat cheese
2 apples
3 tbsp honey
1 tbsp lemon juice
3 ½ tbsp (50 ml) apple cider vinegar
1 tsp finely chopped rosemary
1 tbsp walnut oil + 4 tbsp corn oil or 5 tbsp olive oil
salt and freshly ground black pepper
½ cup (100 ml) walnuts
1 head of frisée lettuce, or baby greens
bread, for serving

☞ Preheat the oven to 400°F (200°C). Slice the cheese into slices about half an inch thick (1 cm). Core and slice the apple. Place the apple slices on a baking sheet lined with parchment paper and place goat cheese slices on top.

☞ Mix the honey with lemon juice, vinegar, and rosemary. Spoon half of the mixture over the apple and goat cheese slices, distributed evenly.

☞ Bake at the top of the oven for about 10 minutes, until the cheese is golden. Combine the rest of the honey and vinegar marinade with oil, salt, and pepper. Roast the walnuts in a dry pan for a few minutes.

☞ Rinse the greens and separate the leaves. Layer the greens with apples and goat cheese. Pour the dressing and walnuts on top. Serve with bread.

DUCK CONFIT WITH FRIED POTATOES

You've just got to try this! Confit de canard is duck legs, prepared by cooking them in their own juices over low heat. You can buy duck legs in well-stocked grocery stores. Nothing is more delicious than crispy duck legs with potatoes fried in the duck fat. The smell that spreads throughout the kitchen—oh là là!

★ ★ ★ ★ ★

4 people

4 duck confits (confit de canard)
2 lbs (1 kg) firm potatoes
1 garlic clove, minced
salt
2 tbsp minced parsley
salad with vinaigrette, for serving

➤ Heat up a pan and fry the duck legs in a bit of fat until crisp on both sides, about 5–8 minutes.

➤ Peel the potatoes and boil them until tender. Cut into slices about half an inch thick (1 cm). Fry the potato slices in the duck fat and add garlic near the end. Add salt and sprinkle parsley on top. Serve the duck legs with the fried potatoes, salad, and vinaigrette.

ENDIVE SALAD WITH ROQUEFORT AND PEARS

Don't be scared away by the slightly bitter flavor that endives can have. With the sweet pear and tangy cheese, the bitterness of the endive will balance out perfectly.

★ ★ ★ ★ ★

4 people

2 endives
2 pears
2 oz (50 g) Roquefort
2 oz (50 g) walnuts

Dressing:
4 tbsp extra virgin olive oil
2 tbsp red wine vinegar
salt and freshly ground black pepper

➤ Cut one or two inches off the bottom of each endive. Pull off the leaves. Peel, core, and slice the pears into small pieces. Crumble the cheese into small pieces. Roast the walnuts until golden-brown, a few minutes, in a dry frying pan.

➤ Mix together the ingredients for the dressing. Arrange the endive leaves with the pears and cheese. Pour over the dressing and scatter the walnuts on top.

WARM SALAD WITH DUCK, CHERRIES, AND HONEY

I came up with this salad when I was hungry for some duck. It wasn't easy to find good duck breast. but I found a few in a small market. Went home. browned them in butter with a touch of cloves. What to do with them? Made this superb salad with cherries in a Port wine sauce. Yum!

4 people

4 duck breasts
1 tbsp butter
salt and freshly ground black pepper
1 pinch freshly ground white pepper
1 pinch ground cloves
1 tbsp freshly squeezed lemon juice
7 fl oz (200 ml) Port or Madeira wine
2 tbsp honey
½ cup (100 ml) pitted cherries
3½ oz (100 g) haricots
verts or green beans
1 head of any salad green, e.g., fri-sée lettuce
1 package of mâche lettuce
bread, for serving

➣ Preheat the oven to 350°F (175°C). Cut the duck breast out of the fat in a square-like shape. Heat the butter in a pan and season the meat on both sides with salt, pepper, and cloves. Brown the duck breasts on both sides in the pan, then transfer them to a baking sheet and place them in the oven for 15–20 minutes. Poke them—they should still feel somewhat resilient when touched lightly. In France, the preferred way to cook and serve duck breast is when it's still light pink on the inside.

➣ Remove the duck, place it on a dish, and cover it with foil. Pour the juices into a saucepan and collect any leftover fat with a spoon. Add the lemon juice, Port wine, and honey. Reduce to obtain a thick, syrupy sauce. Add the cherries and let them heat up; season with salt and pepper to taste and pour into a bowl.

➣ Boil the haricots verts for a few minutes in lightly salted water. They should still be crisp. Then, rinse them in cold water, and mix them with the various greens. Slice the meat thinly and plate it alongside the vegetables. Spoon the cherry-infused gravy on top and serve with bread.

★ ★ ★ ★ ★

RACK OF LAMB WITH BASIL SAUCE

Imagine delicious, juicy meat that melts in your mouth. And with that, pistou—an aromatic, herbal paste with fresh basil, garlic, and some of the best olive oil. A ratatouille gratin is excellent on the side—a marriage of flavors that truly tastes like Provence.

4 people

2 racks of lamb
1 bunch basil
1–2 garlic cloves
3½ tbsp (50 ml)
extra virgin olive oil
salt and freshly
ground black pepper
2 tbsp butter

On the side:
Ratatouille gratin,
see page 64

Place the racks of lamb on a baking sheet. Mince the basil and garlic. Mix with the oil, salt, and pepper. Rub the racks with about half of the pistou.

Preheat the oven to 350°F (175°C). Heat the butter in a pan and sear the meat until golden-brown, a few minutes, on each side. Finish cooking the meat in the oven for about 10–15 minutes, depending on how well done you like your lamb.

Slice the meat and drizzle the rest of the pistou on top. Serve with the ratatouille gratin.

CHICKEN WITH LAVENDER HONEY AND LEMON SAUCE

Lavender has an aromatic taste and is an exciting seasoning that pairs excellently with chicken. Oven-baked chicken with a thick and sticky honey sauce, seasoned simply with lavender and lemon!

4 people

4 fresh chicken legs, with thighs
salt and freshly ground black pepper
1 sprig thyme
1 sprig rosemary
4 tbsp honey, preferably lavender honey
2 tbsp lemon juice
1 tbsp lemon zest
2 tbsp olive oil
1 pinch dried lavender
3½ tbsp (50 g) butter
½ cup (100 ml) white wine
rice or bread and salad for serving

➤ Preheat the oven to 350°F (175°C). Cut the chicken legs into two pieces. Salt and pepper them all around. Mince the thyme and rosemary, and rub them onto the chicken.

➤ Mix the honey, lemon juice, lemon zest, and oil in a bowl. Place the chicken pieces in the mixture and stir them around, then put them on a baking sheet and pour over the marinade. Cook in the middle of the oven for about 45 minutes, until the chicken falls off the bone and the juices run clear. If the chicken starts to brown too much, place a sheet of parchment paper on top and continue cooking until the chicken is done.

➤ Pour the juices into a saucepan and add the lavender, butter (cut into cubes), and white wine. Reduce to a thick, syrupy sauce and season with salt and pepper, to taste.

➤ Serve with rice or bread and vegetables, e.g., a salad or haricots verts.

ENTRECÔTE ET DES ACCOMPAGNEMENTS DIFFÉRENTS

ENTRECÔTE WITH VARIOUS ACCOMPANIMENTS

A good steak never goes amiss. Especially with my delicious sides. Here, I've made two kinds of butter, as well as the classic béarnaise sauce. Café de Paris butter is spicy, with fine, full-bodied flavors. The red wine butter came about when I was experimenting in the kitchen and wanted to find a tasty way to combine butter and red wine.

★ ★ ★ ★ ★

4 pieces of rib eye, 7 oz (200 g) each
salt and freshly ground black pepper
2 tbsp olive oil + 1 tbsp butter

Café de Paris butter:
5⅓ oz (150 g) butter,
room temperature
1 tsp tomato purée
1 tsp Dijon mustard
1 shallot, finely chopped
1 garlic clove, minced
1 tbsp minced parsley
1 tbsp minced tarragon
1 tbsp minced chervil
½ tsp powdered paprika
½ tsp curry powder
1 pinch cayenne pepper
1 tsp Worcestershire sauce
1 tbsp cognac
salt and black pepper

Red wine butter:
2 shallots, finely chopped
½ cup (100 ml) red wine
1 tsp honey
5⅓ oz (150 g) butter, room
temperature
salt and black pepper

Sauce béarnaise:
1 shallot, minced
2 tbsp white wine vinegar or
sherry vinegar
1 tbsp minced fresh tarragon

2 egg yolks
approx. 9 oz (250 g) butter, room temperature
salt and freshly ground black pepper

Glazed rutabaga:
1 rutabaga
3½ tbsp (50 g) butter
2 tbsp veal stock
1 tbsp raw sugar
salt and freshly ground black pepper

➤ Start with the Café de Paris butter. Place the butter in a bowl. Add the tomato purée and Dijon mustard; mix. Then add the shallot, garlic, herbs, spices, Worcestershire sauce, and cognac. Finish with a pinch of salt and a few twists of the pepper grinder. Mix together and place in the fridge for a while to let the flavors develop.

➤ Next, the red wine butter: Mix the shallots, red wine, and honey in a saucepan. Reduce the liquid until there are about two tablespoons left. Set aside to cool. Cut the butter into small cubes and put it in a bowl. Pour the red wine mixture over the butter and whisk to form the sauce. Season with salt and pepper. Place in the fridge for a while to let the flavors develop.

➤ Sauce béarnaise: Place the finely chopped shallot in a saucepan with the vinegar and tarragon. Reduce until only a few tablespoons of liquid are left. Take the saucepan off of the heat and whisk in the egg yolks. Place the saucepan over a water bath and cut the butter into small cubes. Add the butter, a bit at a time, while whisking vigorously until the sauce has thickened. Season with salt and pepper, to taste.

➤ Glazed rutabaga: Peel and dice the rutabaga into small cubes. Heat the butter in a saucepan and sauté the rutabaga, uncovered, until it begins to take on some color. Add the veal stock and the sugar. Season with a bit of salt and black pepper. Continue cooking until the rutabaga is soft and is covered with a shiny, dark sauce.

➤ Season the meat evenly on both sides. Sear it for about 3 minutes on each side in oil and butter. Then let it rest for about 5 minutes. Serve with the butters or sauce and the glazed rutabaga. Pommes frites are a great side, too!

DARING FLAVORS!

Snails, sweetbreads, liver, and stew thickened with pig's blood. Unusual and exciting recipes that I hope you'll be adventurous enough to try. Go on, I dare you!

SNAILS WITH GARLIC AND PARSLEY

Snails with their shells are available in ready-made kits in some well-stocked markets. Poke the snail in with a wooden stick and fill it generously with garlic butter. Cook in the oven to heavenly goodness and eat to your heart's content. Don't forget to dip some bread in the delicious butter.

4 PEOPLE

48 snails with shells
3 shallots
2 garlic cloves
1 small sprig of parsley
2 tbsp white wine
salt and freshly ground black pepper
10½ oz (300 g) butter, room temperature
baguette, for serving

· Set the oven to broil, 475°F (250°C). Place the snails and shells on a baking pan, preferably one made for snails with little indents to set them in. Otherwise, a smaller pan with edges that the shells can rest against will work just as well
· Peel and mince the shallots and garlic. Mince the parsley. Mix the shallots, garlic, parsley, and wine in a deep dish. Season with salt and pepper. Stir in the butter with a fork. This is easiest when the butter is nice and soft.
· Push the snails back into their shell and dab in the garlic butter. Place the snails on the tray with the openings of the shells pointing upwards. Cook in the middle of the oven for about 6–8 minutes until the butter bubbles and gets a touch of color to it. Serve straight out of the pan with baguette and use toothpicks to eat the snails. Dip the bread in the delicious garlic butter.

SWEETBREADS WITH MADEIRA SAUCE

When I was growing up, we often ate sweetbreads. Mom loved to make these for my brother and me. Perhaps it's a bit out there—but you won't be disappointed.

4 PEOPLE

1¼ lbs (600 g) sweetbreads
2 tsp salt
2 tbsp wheat flour
salt and freshly ground white pepper
2 tbsp butter
3½ oz (100 g) mushrooms
¾ cup (200 ml) Madeira wine
2 tbsp veal stock
salad and bread, for serving

· Rinse the sweetbreads in cold water. Place them in a saucepan and pour in enough cold water to cover them. Salt, and bring to a simmer. Skim off the foam with a strainer or spoon. Simmer the sweetbreads for about 8 minutes. Rinse them once again with cold water, and remove all the membranes with a sharp knife. Then, cut the sweetbreads into smaller pieces.
· Mix the flour with salt and pepper in a bowl. Dry the sweetbreads with a dish towel, and set them in the flour mixture. Stir carefully with a spoon, so that the sweetbreads are covered completely by the flour. Shake off any excess flour and place the sweetbreads in a dish.
· Heat the butter in a pan. Sear the sweetbreads for a few minutes until golden brown on all sides. Slice the mushrooms and place them in the pan. Allow everything to warm up. Then pour in the Madeira and stock. Reduce to a thick consistency for about 30–40 minutes, uncovered. Stir every so often to prevent burning. Season with salt and pepper to taste; serve with salad and bread.

★★★★★

CIVET DE PORC OU FRICASSÉE DE CAÏON

STEW WITH PORK LOIN MARINATED IN RED WINE

This stew takes a while to make, so start well in advance—the meat needs to marinate for at least 12 hours. To thicken the stew, you use pig's blood. Don't be scared; it adds both flavor and character to the dish. My friend Laurent Laffont grew up in Grenoble, where this is a favorite way to eat pork.

4 PEOPLE

2 lbs (1 kg) pork loin or pork jowl (gu-
anciale)
7 oz (200 g) lightly salted pork belly
1½ yellow onion
2 whole cloves
1 carrot
1 bouquet garni (tie together parsley
leaves, thyme, two pieces of leek tops,
and a bay leaf with cooking twine)
4¼ cups (1 liter) red wine (e.g., Côtes
du Rhône)

2 tbsp butter or duck fat
2 tbsp sunflower oil
3 tbsp wheat flour
1 tsp salt
1 tsp white pepper
½ cup (100 ml) pig's blood

POLENTA
3 cups (700 ml) milk
1¼ cups (300 ml) water
¾ cup (200 ml) cornmeal
2 tbsp butter
¼ tsp nutmeg
¼ tsp salt
¼ tsp white pepper
1 egg yolk

• Slice the pork loin into 1½-inch (4 cm) pieces, and cut the pork belly into cubes of about the same size. Peel one onion and chop the entire thing into small pieces; roast the half onion in a frying pan over high heat so it becomes somewhat blackened. Press the whole cloves into the half onion. Peel and slice the carrot into small pieces. Place the meat, all the onions, the carrots, and the bouquet garni in a bowl. Pour the wine on top. Cover, then place in the fridge and let it marinate for at least 12 hours—preferably longer.
• Continue by preparing the polenta. Bring the milk and water to a boil. Add the cornmeal, butter, and spices. Simmer on low heat for 10 minutes, stirring the entire time. Take the saucepan off the heat and stir in the egg yolks. Line a small plan with plastic wrap, and pour in the polenta. Place in the fridge to harden.
• Remove the meat and allow it to drain. Save the liquid and vegetables. Heat the butter and oil in a saucepan. Sear the meat on all sides on high heat for a few minutes. Add the flour, salt, and pepper while continuing to stir; the flour should turn light brown. Add the liquid from the marinade with herbs and vegetables, but take out the half onion with cloves in it and toss it out. Allow the contents of the pan to come to a boil. If the liquid doesn't quite cover the meat, add a bit of water or wine. Skim the surface thoroughly and simmer for about an hour and a half with the lid left slightly open.
• Remove the herb bouquet and throw it out. When the meat feels tender, add the blood and reduce to form a thick sauce. If the stock is too thick, dilute it a bit with water. Cut the polenta into small pieces and fry them in butter until golden-brown; serve them with the stew.

LAURENT'S VEAL LIVER WITH RAISINS

I'll admit that I'm not a huge fan of the organs. But, my French friend Laurent and I took a culinary journey and tried a wide range of foods until we discovered this yummy dish. It was surprisingly good! The rich, juicy veal liver is combined perfectly with both raisins and raspberry vinegar, giving it a nice touch of sweetness.

4 PEOPLE

½ cup (100 ml) raisins
½ cup (100 ml) white wine
¾ cup (200 ml) small peas
1 shallot
14 oz (400 g) veal liver
salt and white pepper
butter, for pan-frying
2 tbsp raspberry vinegar
1 tbsp butter
salt and white pepper
boiled potatoes or salad and bread, for serving

· Pour the raisins into a bowl and pour the wine over top. Let the raisins soak up the wine for at least 30 minutes. Warm the peas in a bit of water. Peel and thinly slice the shallot.

· Cut the veal liver into slices about half an inch (1 cm) thick. Salt and pepper both sides. Heat the butter in a pan and fry until golden-brown, a few minutes on each side. Place in a dish off to the side.

· Next, make the sauce: put the raisins and their marinade into the pan with the raspberry vinegar. Let it reduce to a thick, syrupy sauce. Add 1 tbsp of butter and whisk together so the sauce becomes nice and shiny.

· Place the liver in the sauce and let everything warm up. Season with salt and pepper to taste. Arrange the liver pieces on plates with the peas and shallot. Spoon the sauce on top. Boiled potatoes are good on the side, as is salad and bread.

ON CHEESE

Where to begin? It's said that there are several hundred different kinds of cheese in France. They're all delicious, too. They're typically divided into fresh cheeses, hard cheeses, white mold cheeses, goat cheeses, washed-rind cheeses, and bleu cheeses.

My favorite is probably the aged hard cheese, comté. Mild and with a nutty flavor, it really speaks to me.

Here, we're dealing with regional products, each and every one from its own terroir. For example, a goat cheese can take on many different forms depending on where it's made—conical, rolled in ashes, small and round, or oblong. All with different tastes and characteristics. Unfortunately, due to restrictions on unpasteurized milk products, authentic French cheeses are not always available for international sale.

Authentic Roquefort cheese comes from the damp Combalou caves in the city of Roquefort-sur-Soulzon, where it is aged.

In France, people always eat cheese before dessert. Often, three different kinds. A good combination to start with is a bit of brie, goat cheese, and bleu cheese or highly aged comté. Bread and wine, naturally, go well with the cheese.

Sainte-Maure de Touraine

Saint-Marcellin

Roquefort

"Un repas sans fromage est une belle à qui il manque un œil."

➤ If you love creamy cheeses with a bite to them, you've got to try Saint Marcellin. This white mold cheese from Rhône-Alpes is small, but oh so good.

➤ Roquefort is a famous sheep's milk cheese with a distinct character. Legend tells of a shepherd who, in one of the caves of Mont Combalou, forgot his sheep cheese. When he came back later, it had become bleu cheese.

➤ In French cheese shops, there's more than one kind of goat cheese to choose from: oblong, conical, round, and with different characteristics and flavors. Sainte-Maure de Touraine has a fresh, tart taste and is rolled in ash.

➤ A beautiful, orange washed-rind cheese with a wavy exterior. Langres has a rich flavor and is delightfully creamy. It's a fine, mild cow's milk cheese from Champagne.

➤ A creamy white mold cheese that's well-known and well-liked, Brie de Meaux is without a doubt the king of the cheese platter.

➤ Gruyère, with its nutty flavor, is my favorite. Here, you might also choose a comté from Jura or another alpine cheese aged for at least a year.

Langres

Brie de Meaux

Gruyère

SWEETS

In France, people are very, very fond of
desserts. They round out meals and perk
you up with something sweet after the
main course and the cheese. I personally
have a preference for desserts that aren't
too sweet. That's why I make my chocolate
mousse sinfully dark, and why I choose a
marinated fruit salad with rum to go along
with the sticky chocolatey-goodness. Mille-
feuille is an exciting classic made with
thin, flaky puff pastry that I fill with
apricots and cream, flavored with lemon
zest and vanilla. Then there're my red
wine-poached pears, which are so
wonderfully beautiful. Stay up late and
enjoy a good dessert—la vie est belle!

LAYERED PASTRY WITH APRICOTS

Crispy layers of puff pastry filled with tender, juicy apricots get an extra kick from a tangy syrup. In between, there's whipped cream with lemon zest and vanilla for extra flavor. What can I say?—it's a dessert I can't get enough of. Such heavenly goodness!

4 PEOPLE

¼ cup (50 ml) powdered sugar
1 package of fresh puff pastry, or
2 frozen slabs

FILLING

7 oz (200 g) fresh apricots
¼ cup (50 ml) sugar
2–3 tbsp water
1 tbsp lemon juice

VANILLA AND LEMON CREAM

½ cup (100 ml) powdered sugar
1 vanilla bean or 1 tsp vanilla extract
½ lemon, zest and juice
1¼ cups (300 ml) whipping cream

2 tbsp powdered sugar, for serving

• Preheat the oven to 400°F (200°C). Line a baking sheet with parchment paper. Using a sifter, dust the parchment paper with half of the powdered sugar. Roll out the puff pastry as thin as possible on a lightly floured surface. Cut out eight rectangles, about 2½ x 5 inches (6 x 12 cm). Place the dough pieces on the baking sheet and dust them with the rest of the powdered sugar. Prick the pastry sheets with a fork. Bake in the middle of the oven for about 12–15 minutes—make sure they don't burn. Remove the baking sheet and place another sheet of parchment paper on top. Immediately place a second baking sheet on top of this and press down. Let sit for a while to cool.

• Cut the apricots into halves and remove the pit. Bring the sugar, water, and lemon juice to a boil. Set the fruit in the boiling mixture and allow it to be heated through. Then leave it to cool while covered.

• Now prepare the vanilla and lemon cream: Pour the powdered sugar into a bowl. Cut open the vanilla bean and scrape the seeds into the bowl or add the vanilla extract. Add the lemon zest, lemon juice, and cream. Whisk until fluffy.

• Here comes the fun part. Place each of four finished puff pastry sheets on its own small plate. Top with the vanilla and citrus cream and apricots. Finish each one off with a second layer of pastry, then more cream and apricots. Spoon a bit of the syrup the apricots cooked in on top, then dust with powdered sugar.

LEMON TART

Lemons are always in my kitchen at home—a favorite ingredient that I just can't do without. They have a wonderful, fresh sourness that's lovely in a creamy tart that might otherwise be too heavy and sweet. Delightfully delicious, citrusy lemon tart that simply melts in your mouth. Mmm . . .

6–8 PEOPLE

DOUGH

7 tbsp (100 g) butter, room temperature
1 ½ cups (350 ml) wheat flour
1 egg yolk
1 tbsp powdered sugar
1 tbsp cold water

FILLING

5 eggs, preferably organic
4 organic lemons
1 tbsp lemon zest
½ cup (100 ml) whipping cream
½ cup (100 ml) granulated sugar

powdered sugar, for decorating
whipped cream, for serving, optionally

• Preheat the oven to 350°F (175°C). Start by making the dough. Mix the butter, flour, egg yolk, powdered sugar, and water. Knead together with a light touch to form a smooth dough. Press out the dough in a spring-form pan, about 9½ inches (24 cm) in diameter. Pre-bake the crust for about 10 minutes until it's a light golden color. Take it out and let it cool.

• Meanwhile, make the filling: whisk together the eggs in a bowl. Squeeze in the juice from the lemons, and grate 1 tbsp of lemon zest into the bowl. Add the whipping cream and sugar, then whisk thoroughly.

• Fill the cooled crust with the lemon cream and cook the tart for about 30 minutes, until the cream has set and feels a bit firm. Allow the tart to cool, and decorate it with the powdered sugar. Good on its own, or with whipped cream.

OVEN PANCAKE WITH CHERRIES

*A French style oven pancake is typically fil-
led with plum. It has a light consistency,
since the egg yolks and whites are whisked
separately before being combined in a fluffy
batter. I make my clafoutis in small ramekins and fill them with juicy cherries.*

4 PEOPLE

*2 cups (½ liter) cherries
4 eggs
½ cup (100 ml) sugar + 4 tbsp sugar
1 pinch salt
½ cup (100 ml) milk
½ cup (100 ml) cream
1 vanilla bean or 1 tsp vanilla extract
½ cup (100 ml) wheat flour
2 tbsp butter
2 tbsp raw sugar
optionally, whipped cream, for serving*

• Preheat the oven to 400°F (200°C). Remove the
seeds from the cherries. Separate the egg yolks from
the whites. Whisk the yolks until thick and puffy in a
bowl, along with ½ cup (100 ml) sugar. Add 4 tbsp
sugar and a pinch of salt to the egg whites. Then
whisk them into a stiff, glossy foam. Pour the milk
and cream into the yolks and stir. Cut open the vanilla bean and scrape out the seeds. Add the vanilla
seeds or the vanilla extract, and the flour. Blend
thoroughly together, and then add in the egg whites.
• Butter the small ramekins or a larger dish. Coat the
inside with the raw sugar. Put in the pitted cherries,
and pour in the egg batter. Cook in the middle of the
oven for about 15 minutes (for small ramekins) or 25
minutes (for a big dish). If the surface begins to
brown too much, cover it with a sheet of parchment
paper. Serve with fluffy whipped cream, or as is.

CHOCOLATE MOUSSE WITH FRUIT SALAD IN RUM SYRUP

I like my chocolate mousse dark and fluffy. It should melt in your mouth and be made from proper, high quality chocolate. A sweet and citrusy fruit salad complements the smooth, soft chocolatey-goodness nicely.

4 PEOPLE

5 ⅓ oz (150 g) high quality dark chocolate, 70% cacao

4 eggs

¼ cup (50 ml) sugar

1 pinch salt

FRUIT SALAD

3½ oz (100 g) cherries

1 pear

2 nectarines

1 melon, e.g., cantaloupe

1 vanilla bean or 1 tsp vanilla extract

1 tbsp powdered sugar

1 tbsp freshly squeezed lemon juice

2 tbsp rum

· Break the chocolate into small pieces in a bowl. Melt it slowly over a water bath. Place to the side and let it cool a bit.

· Separate the egg yolks and whites. Whisk the yolks with the sugar into a light, yet thick consistency. Slowly stir the melted chocolate into the egg batter.

· Whisk the egg whites with a pinch of salt into a light and fluffy foam. Carefully add it to the chocolate batter. Pour into portion-sized glasses and place in the fridge so that the mousse can set.

· Halve and pit the cherries. Peel and slice the pear into smaller pieces. Remove the pit from the nectarine and slice it into chunks. Slice the melon down the middle, remove the seeds and stringy center, and slice it into chunks as well. Mix all the fruit in a bowl. Slice open the vanilla bean and scrape out the seeds into the fruit salad, or add the vanilla extract. Add the powdered sugar, lemon juice, and rum; stir well. Serve the chocolate mousse with the fruit salad.

MANGO SORBET WITH PINEAPPLE, CARAMEL SYRUP, AND SEA SALT

This dessert has a beautiful mixture of sweet, sour, and salty. Sorbet is really delicious after a heavy meal. Mixed together with pineapple and a creamy caramel sauce, it's an exciting dessert that I think you ought to try right away.

4 PEOPLE

½ fresh pineapple
1 tbsp butter
1 pint (500 g) mango sorbet
sea salt

CARAMEL SAUCE
½ cup (100 ml)
raw sugar
2 tbsp water
¼ cup (50 ml)
whipping cream
3½ tbsp (50 g) butter

• Peel and slice the pineapple into quarters. Cut away the core. Cut into slices. Heat the butter in a pan and lightly brown the pineapple pieces on both sides.

• Now, make the caramel sauce: pour the sugar and water into a saucepan over medium heat. Stir until the sugar has dissolved. Add the whipping cream and continue cooking the mixture to achieve a thick consistency. Dollop in the butter and allow it to cool for a while.

• Spoon the mango sorbet into glasses and fill them the rest of the way with the pineapple. Drizzle with the caramel sauce and top with a bit of sea salt.

CRÈME BRÛLÉE

What a wonderful bistro classic! Smooth, creamy custard under a crispy sugar coating. It's easiest to prepare the crème a day in advance. Bake it in the oven, and store it in the fridge. Just before serving, add a layer of caramelized sugar. Then you'll have the perfect brûlée, where the cool custard meets the warm, crispy caramel on top—so unbelievably tasty.

★ ★ ★ ★ ★

4 PEOPLE

1¾ cups (400 ml) whipping cream
1 vanilla bean or 1 tsp vanilla extract
½ cup (100 ml) sugar
4 egg yolks
4 tbsp raw sugar

· Preheat the oven to 350°F (175°C). Pour the cream into a saucepan Slice open the vanilla bean and scrape the seeds and bean into the pan or add the vanilla extract. Add the sugar to the cream. Whisk and allow it to come to a boil. Add the egg yolks and whisk the batter together. Simmer over low heat until the batter thickens; it'll take a few minutes. The mixture should stick to the back of a spoon.
· Take the saucepan off the heat and remove the vanilla bean. Pour the cream mixture into ramekins for baking. Place them in a small baking dish and fill it halfway with water. Cook in the middle of the oven for about 40–45 minutes until the custard has set but is still somewhat runny in the center. Allow the brûlée to cool. If you can, place the molds in the fridge overnight.
· Take the molds out of the fridge shortly before it's time to eat, and scatter the raw sugar over the top. Heat with a kitchen blowtorch until the sugar has become a beautiful brown color. Alternatively, place the molds in the oven and set it to broil, 475°F (250°C), for a few minutes, with the oven door open. Be careful not to burn the sugar.

～ APPLE TART ～

A classic upside-down apple tart—I like to make mine in a cast-iron pan. Apple slices simmer in butter and sugar until they're transparent and tender. Then they're topped with puff pastry and finished off in the oven. It's important to use firm apples, or you'll end up with mush.

8–10 PIECES

²⁄₃ cup (150 ml) raw sugar
1 tbsp lemon juice
3½ tbsp (50 g) butter
5 firm apples
1 egg
1 roll of puff pastry dough

VANILLA CRÈME
7 fl oz (200 ml) crème fraîche
or sour cream
2 tbsp powdered sugar
1 vanilla bean or 1 tsp
vanilla extract

• Preheat the oven to 400°F (200°C). Place an oven-safe pan on the stove and melt the sugar, lemon juice, and butter together to achieve a thick consistency. The mixture should be golden brown.

• Peel and core the apples, then slice them thinly. Place them in the butter and sugar mixture. Let them simmer for 7–8 minutes.

• Crack the egg and whisk it lightly. Roll out the puff pastry and place it on top of the pan like a lid. Cut away any extra dough. Brush with the egg and bake in the middle of the oven for about 30 minutes, until the tart takes on a nice color. Reduce the heat toward the end or cover the tart with a sheet of parchment paper so it doesn't get too dark.

• Take out the pan and carefully cut around the edge. Place a dish over the pan and rapidly turn the whole thing upside down. Lift away the pan.

• Whisk the crème fraîche and powdered sugar together. Slice the vanilla bean open, scrape the seeds into the crème or add the vanilla extract, and mix. Serve the tart at room temperature with the vanilla crème.

POIRES AU VIN ROUGE ET
★ CRÈME DE NOISETTE ★

RED WINE-POACHED PEARS WITH HAZELNUT CRÈME

I'm really quite fond of this beautiful and sensuous dessert. It's delicious and comforting when the weather starts to get cold. Simmer the pears with red wine and honey—then reduce the liquid to a syrupy consistency, and drizzle it over the pears. Serve with whipped cream and roasted hazelnuts. You can prepare the pears a day in advance if you'd like.

4 PEOPLE

4 firm pears

SYRUP
2 cups (500 ml) red wine
1 tbsp honey
¼ cup (50 ml) raw sugar

HAZELNUT CRÈME
3½ oz (100 g) hazelnuts
2 cups (200 ml) whipping cream
1 tsp sugar

· Peel the pears, but leave the stems in place. Pack them tightly into a saucepan. Pour in the wine, honey, and sugar. Simmer, covered, over low heat until the pears are soft, which should take about 20 minutes. Remove the pears and set them aside. Simmer the mixture uncovered for about 5 minutes to obtain a syrupy consistency.
· Roast the hazelnuts until golden-brown in a dry frying pan. Mix them well. Whisk the cream and sugar until fluffy. Mix the cream with the hazelnuts and serve them with the pears at room temperature. Top it off by drizzling the red wine syrup on top.

TARTE AMANDINE AUX POIRES

ALMOND TART WITH PEARS

Oh là là, what a tart! The French are very skilled when it comes to different kinds of tarts. I particularly like this one, with crunchy almonds and sweet pears.

8–10 PEOPLE

DOUGH
1¼ cups (300 ml)
wheat flour
7 tbsp (100 g) butter
2 tbsp cold water

FILLING
4 ripe pears
½ cup (100 ml) almonds
2 eggs
½ cup (100 ml) sugar
½ cup (100 ml) crème
fraîche or sour cream
1 lemon

ON THE SIDE
¾ cup (200 ml) crème
fraîche or sour cream
¼ cup (50 ml) powdered
sugar

• Preheat the oven to 400°F (200°C). Mix the flour and butter together to form a grainy mass. Add water and quickly work into a smooth dough. Allow the dough to rest for 30 minutes or so in the fridge. Then, press it out into a springform pan or any other pie pan with a diameter of about 9½ inches (24 cm). Pre-bake the crust in the middle of the oven for about 10 minutes, or until it's got just a hint of color to it.

• Peel and slice the pears in halves. Remove the cores and arrange them in an attractive pattern in the crust. Roast the almonds in a dry frying pan for a few minutes—until they take on some color and pop in the pan. Mix them thoroughly. Whisk together the eggs, sugar, and crème fraîche. Zest the lemon while avoiding the white pith, which tastes bitter. Stir the lemon zest and almonds into the batter. Pour the mixture over the pears.

• Bake in the middle of the oven until the tart has set and is nicely browned. This should take about 25–30 minutes.

• Blend the crème fraîche and powdered sugar together; serve ice-cold with the warm tart.

HAZELNUT AND CHOCOLATE CRÈME

Hazelnut and chocolate is an unbeatable combination that I downright love. My kids do too! Here, I've blended the two flavors into a rich and dangerously delicious crème, which my kids love to eat on baguette dipped in hot chocolate. I prefer it on a croissant, dipped in café au lait.

1 JAR

½ cup (100 ml) Nutella
7 oz (200 g) dark chocolate, 70% cacao
3½ tbsp (50 g) butter
¼ cup (50 ml) cream
2 tbsp molasses
1 tbsp water
3½ oz (100 g) hazelnuts

· Place the Nutella in a saucepan. Coarsely chop up the chocolate and place it in the pan. Cut the butter into small pieces and add it too, along with the cream, molasses, and water. Warm over low heat to make a smooth sauce. Move the saucepan off to one side.

· Roast the nuts in a dry pan for 3–4 minutes. Mix them well and blend them into the sauce. Pour the crème into a jar with a tight lid. If stored in the fridge, it should keep for at least one week.

SOUPE FROIDE DE NECTARINE
ICE-COLD NECTARINE SOUP

★ ★ ★ ★ ★

*I enjoyed this dessert on a warm
summer day in France. It's best when
the nectarines are good and ripe.
Simply mix pitted nectarines with
lemon and a bit of sugar. I find this to
be a great way to use fruit for a light,
fresh dessert.*

4 PEOPLE

*6 ripe nectarines
½ lemon
2 tbsp powdered sugar*

· Pit the nectarines. Slice them into coarse
chunks and place them in a food processor or
blender. Squeeze in the lemon juice and pour
in the powdered sugar. Blend into a smooth
soup. Pour into a glass and place in the fridge.
Serve ice-cold.

★ CRÊPES AU CITRON ★
CRÊPES WITH LEMON SUGAR

★ ★ ★ ★ ★

*What would a French cookbook be
without crêpes? Those soft, buttery, and
thin pancakes you can buy just about
anywhere in France. So simple and
delicious with just freshly squeezed
lemon and raw sugar on top . . . or filled
with my amazingly good noisette crème.*

4 PEOPLE

*3 eggs
1¼ cups (300 ml) wheat flour
3½ tbsp (50 g) butter, melted
1 pinch salt
1 cup (250 ml) milk, 2%
1 cup (250 ml) cold water
butter, for pan-frying*

*2 lemons, cut into wedges
½ cup (100 ml) raw sugar*

· Whisk the eggs until fluffy. Add the flour
gradually and continue whisking until all
clumps have disappeared. Add the butter and
salt; whisk together. Finally, pour in the milk
and water, and whisk the mixture into a runny pancake batter. Place in the fridge to cool
for at least an hour.
· Pour a thin layer of batter into a frying-pan
with butter, and cook until it takes on a light
golden color. Serve with sugar and lemon.

DRINKS

Start with the best of the best: a glass of ice-cold champagne, with fizzy bubbles and tinglingly good flavor.

Dinner starts with an apéritif or apéro. Sweet red wines, sherry, or light white wines are also good introductions.

If you ask me, wine is the perfect companion to a well-cooked meal. You could write a whole new book about wine pairings, so I'll just settle for a few tips. Round, buttery white wines like chablis pair well with Sole beurre blanc. Light, fruity rosé wines pair well with charcuterie and young, freshly harvested vegetables. Distinct red, round tones for Bœuf bourguignon.

The meal comes to a close with a digestif. Heavier, rich, dark drinks that aid digestion make for a fine ending to a festive dinner. Cognac and liqueurs, or my delectable coffee drink, Café parisienne with orange liqueur. Oh là là! Je t'aime, Paris!

COFFEE WITH ORANGE LIQUEUR AND CREAM

Almost like a dessert, with strong coffee and sweet liqueur with notes of orange.

1 GLASS

1½ fl oz (40 ml) grand marnier
1 double espresso
2 tbsp cream, lightly whipped
½ tsp cocoa powder

Pour the liquor into the glass. Fill with hot coffee and top with whipped cream. Dust with cocoa powder to finish.

PASTIS

A typical French liqueur with hints of anise and licorice, popular as an apéritif in France.

1 glass

1 fl oz (30 ml) pastis (e.g., pernod)
cold water

Pour the pastis into a tall glass. Serve the cold water in a jug on the side and dilute according to your own tastes. One part pastis to five parts water is a common proportion.

★ KIR ROYAL ★

A glamorous drink with champagne and blackcurrant liqueur.

1 glass

1⅓ fl oz (40 ml) crème de cassis
ice cube
Champagne

Pour the crème de cassis in a glass. Fill with the ice and cold Champagne.

SPRING DINNER
A PICNIC IN THE COUNTRYSIDE

PAIN BAGNA
Street sandwich with tuna and vegetables

★

AMUSE-BOUCHE AU ROQUEFORT ET CÉLERI
Cheese balls with Roquefort and celery

★

TIAN À LA COURGE
Oven-baked omelette with squash

★

Paté or charcuterie, a few different cheeses, and bread

Here are some tips on how you can combine different recipes. Try my tips for different seasons and enjoy a lovely, complete French meal.

QUICK AND SIMPLE DINNER

TAPENADE
Tapenade with cold cuts, cheeses, bread, and olives

★

BOEUF À LA MINUTE
Minute steak with French herbs and salad

or

MOULES
Mussels

★

Fresh fruit and quality chocolate

or, if you prepared the day before:

CRÈME BRÛLÉE

SUMMER DINNER
OUTDOOR GRILLING

CÔTE D'AGNEAU ET PISTOU
Rack of lamb with basil sauce

★

SALADE DE TOMATES ET AUBERGINES
AU FOUR ET FROMAGE DE FETA
*Tomato salad with oven-baked eggplant
and feta cheese*

or

SALADE DE CHÈVRE CHAUD AUX POMMES
Warm goat cheese salad with apple

★

SOUPE FROIDE DE NECTARINE
Ice-cold nectarine soup

or

TARTE AU CITRON
Lemon tart

WARM AND RICH

⁂

CHAMPIGNONS À LA BORDELAISE
Mushrooms with garlic and parsley

★

POT AU FEU
*Chicken stew with clear broth
and vegetables*

★

TARTE TATIN
Apple tart

or

POIRES AU VIN ROUGE ET À LA CRÈME
DE NOISETTE
*Red wine-poached pears with
hazelnut crème*

WHEN THE COLD CREEPS IN

⁂

LÉGUMES À LA GRECQUE
*Vegetables in broth with spices and
white wine*

or

SALADE DE TOMATES ET ORANGES
Tomato and orange salad

★

ESCALOPE DE FOIE DE VEAU AUX RAISINS
À LA LAURENT
Laurent's veal liver with raisins

or

BOEUF BOURGUIGNON
Rich beef stew

★

MOUSSE AU CHOCOLAT ET
SALADE DE FRUITS AU RHUM
*Chocolate mousse with fruit salad
in rum syrup*

ACKNOWLEDGMENTS

My wonderful family! Dearest Ola, thanks for all the support and for always being there. You sought out all sorts of fine props and helped with a ton of other things I could never have managed on my own. Nora and Siri, my beautiful girls who love making food and are always ready to help in the kitchen. You two make the cutest models, too.

★

Mom, dad, and my little brother, Karim. What great food we always ate that I'm now using for inspiration! Thanks for that!

★

Dearest Åsa! The worst best photographer. You're like an injection of vitamins to me. Without you, this book would have never taken off. It's been so much fun! And what an amazing start we had to the book in Paris—that was wonderful. Oh là là, what beautiful pictures!

★

François, Laurent and Helen, Anita, Jill and Sebastian, Annu and Agnes. Thank you all very much for letting me use your homes and items—and for being my extras, helping me to make the book so beautiful!

★

My Swedish publisher Semic: such pep and support! Eva Holmberg, the best editor, and my publisher, Annelie Lindqvist, who believed in me. Monica Sundberg, what design! I'm so incredibly happy to have gotten the chance to make this book. It's been a fantastic trip!

★

Thank you for the impeccably fine ingredients: La Maison Française, Everts Sjöbod (Per, your oysters are world-class . . .), Boulangerie Ducoin, Rökeriet i Strömstad, Sudagatt and franskaoliver.se.

★

Everyone who's been a treasure trove of wonderful props: Logen's Antikt och Vintage, Herbret Antikt, Atmosphere, Majorna's Things from Before, Grandma, Suedeco.se, Bagaren och Kocken, François Augier and Tröts i Strömstad—thank you for the wonderful children's clothes!

RECIPE INDEX